Matty and Matt

Matty and Matt

A Conversational Approach to Matthew's Gospel

SEL CARADUS

RESOURCE *Publications* • Eugene, Oregon

MATTY AND MATT
A Conversational Approach to Matthew's Gospel

Copyright © 2011 Sel Caradus. All rights reserved. Except for brief quotations in critical publications or reviews, no part of this book may be reproduced in any manner without prior written permission from the publisher. Write: Permissions, Wipf and Stock Publishers, 199 W. 8th Ave., Suite 3, Eugene, OR 97401.

Resource Publications
An Imprint of Wipf and Stock Publishers
199 W. 8th Ave., Suite 3
Eugene, OR 97401
www.wipfandstock.com

ISBN 13: 978-1-61097-432-5

Manufactured in the U.S.A.

All scripture quotations, unless otherwise indicated, are taken from the Holy Bible, New International Version®, NIV®. Copyright ©1973, 1978, 1984 by Biblica, Inc.™ Used by permission of Zondervan. All rights reserved worldwide.

This book is dedicated to first time readers of Matthew's Gospel.

Contents

Acknowledgments ix

Preface xi

First Meeting / 1

Chapter 1 / 7

Chapter 2 / 14

Chapter 3 / 18

Chapter 4 / 23

Chapter 5 / 31

Chapter 6 / 41

Chapter 7 / 48

Chapter 8 / 53

Chapter 9 / 59

Chapter 10 / 65

Chapter 11 / 72

Chapter 12 / 79

Chapter 13 / 88

Chapter 14 / 96

Chapter 15 / 102

Chapter 16 / 107

Chapter 17 / 112

Chapter 18 / 118

Chapter 19 / 123

Chapter 20 / 129

Chapter 21 / 135

Chapter 22 / 143

Chapter 23 / 149

Chapter 24 / 154

Chapter 25 / 161

Chapter 26 / 167

Chapter 27 / 176

Chapter 28 / 184

Epilogue / 189

Note: The twenty-eight chapters listed above contain consecutive conversations on the twenty-eight chapters of Matthew's Gospel.

Acknowledgments

Sincere thanks are due to readers of a first draft: Caroline Davis, Daniel Fraikin, David Hawks, Frances MacArthur, Herbert O'Driscoll, Fred Peirce, and Win Perryman. Their encouragement and perceptive comments have helped me nurture a final draft from its uncertain beginnings.

Preface

In his essay, *Kafka at Las Vegas*, Alan Bennett says, "There are many perils in writing about Kafka. His work is garrisoned by armies of critics, with some fifteen thousand books about him at last count. As there is a Castle Freud, so there is a Castle Kafka…For admission, a certain high seriousness must be deemed essential, and I am not sure I have it." I would say much the same about Matthew's Gospel: as there is Castle Freud, so there is Castle Matthew. It is a bold outsider who, having read two, or perhaps three, of the "fifteen thousand books" about Matthew's Gospel, would have the courage to put pen to paper and produce book number fifteen thousand and one!

A different approach is helpful: to put the topic in the form of a conversation among a group of average people, possessed of knowledge which might be obtained from the reading of books obtainable in the local secular bookstore or desultory surfing of the Internet, and united only by a willingness to share insights and/or ignorance. Such an "conversational approach" might be justified by the thought that Gospel texts were not primarily addressed to scholars but to ordinary readers (or, rather, hearers) in the first instance.

Discussions which ensue in such a group will sometimes be inconclusive. Many possibilities can present themselves to the careful reader of a text. Indeed, a glance at one or two commentaries makes the reader aware of the wide variety of opinions held by reputable scholars. Even the most basic questions about Matthew's Gospel are in dispute:

- When was it written and by whom?
- Of the four gospels which begin the New Testament, was it the earliest (as was long thought and as a minority opinion continues to insist) or was it written with Mark's Gospel already available?
- Was there another document, known as "Q", which accounts for those parts of Matthew and Luke which agree but are not found

in Mark? Careers have been made on discussions about "Q" even though its existence is hypothetical!

- Hostility is expressed in Matthew's Gospel by Jesus towards the Jewish group known as the Pharisees. Does this represent the conflict which the early church was having with Jewish opponents or does it record the attitudes of Jesus himself?

- And did the writer of Matthew's Gospel feel free to put words in the mouth of Jesus to represent the theological concerns of the community at the time of writing? (The Jesus Seminar which attracted so much attention for a few years, would argue that few of the words and deeds recorded in any of the canonical Gospels have a basis in historical fact.)

The "conversational approach" can scarcely be expected to enter into such questions. It will leave many matters unsettled. One might not wish to go as far as Flaubert whose aphorism, "Stupidity is the need for conclusions" might discourage inquiry. But there is the more moderate view of John Keats who defined "negative capability" as the state of "being in uncertainties, mysteries and doubts without any irritable reaching after fact and reason."

Those who have never participated in a study group of the kind encountered here might imagine a glum collection of old-fashioned folk, eager to confirm their traditional beliefs. But, in my experience, participants are usually lively and somewhat irreverent; humorous asides are commonplace. They are serious without being solemn.

It goes without saying but needs to be said that the characters encountered in this narrative are not based on any persons, living or dead. Deliberately, details of each are only sketched; this is not a novel and too much emphasis on the personal histories of participants distracts from the main task. Deliberately, much is left unsaid. The Gospel of Matthew, short though it is, provokes intense differences of opinion. It is hoped that readers with some curiosity about Christian scripture but with neither patience nor motivation to tackle heavyweight writings will find something of value.

The entire text of Matthew's Gospel, adapted from the Weymouth translation (1903), is included for the convenience of the reader.

First Meeting

ANXIETY MADE HER LEAVE early and drove faster than her usual careful speed. So it wasn't surprising that she arrived in the parking lot of the Parish Center at 6.50 and by 7.05 p.m., there she was, sitting at the Great Table with PowerPoint plugged in and ready to go. Twenty five minutes of dead time. Time for increased anxiety. If she had been a pious person, she thought, she would have prayed.

Instead, she let her mind roam back to the first time she had sat at that table, in the days when the house had been the Bishop's Residence. Anxiety of a different kind when, as a seventeen year old, she had accompanied her father to a dinner where the Bishop held court. Her chief concern had been to pick up the right fork at the right time and to speak when spoken to. Not that there was much need for conversation from others when the Bishop entertained. He reveled in his power, as the clergy, her father included, deferred to their Father-in-God.

Then, more recently, she'd sat at the same table representing her law firm, party to endless discussion of property transfer, church closings and occasionally, devising defenses against lawsuits.

So her mind wandered until the door opened at 7.15 and Webster Smith showed his weathered face. She knew him well and thought that he would sympathize with her predicament. His first words were reassuring: "Melanie, your aunt would be pleased to see you there. We are all looking forward to an interesting evening." The good old boy spoke without irony. He could be taken at face value but was by no means a fool, though sometimes tedious.

Soon, others were arriving. Most of them she knew at least by sight and some of them she felt she knew rather too well. Aunt Matty's colorful accounts of her sessions with them over the years often provided breakfast table conversation. But they all seemed friendly enough and the very fact that they had signed up again suggested that they were not completely unhappy with her inherited place at the head of the table.

Melanie was pleased that she could greet them by name, all but one. A man, about her own age but unknown to her, came in with a group and she singled him out for introductions around the table. He was Al, an Australian, owner of a local bookstore, but his second name escaped her. He identified himself as a "survivor" of a men's study group which had met the previous year. Some of its difficulties were known, even to her. By choice, she remained outside the parish network of information-sharing which an unkind person might call "gossip". His use of the word, "survivor," seemed unfortunate and she remarked that he had "survived" remarkably well and that he would "find our gatherings very different".

At precisely 7.30, she raised her voice to call them to some kind of order. Aunt Matty's notes had warned her that she had begun the sessions with a prayer, so she called for a moment of silence and then read from a card the "prayer" which she had prepared:

"May we listen with care, speak with charity, differ with respect and in all things, be ready for change. Amen."

It felt strange to be "praying", especially in public. It wasn't much of a prayer but had the virtue of sincerity even though her thoughts about the benefits of prayer were ambivalent on a good day. Especially on a good day!

When they all came back from the "Amen", she looked around the table. They had signed up for this program, (known over the years as "Meetings with Matty"), and cleared their calendars so that, apart from illness, they could be relied upon to appear Tuesday nights, 7.30 to 9.30, for the duration. This was what Aunt Matty insisted on and they seemed willing to transfer that willingness to the new situation.

She had gone to some trouble to prepare preliminary remarks, as though opening in court, hoping that she wouldn't sound too much like a defense counsel.

"Most of you will know the circumstances which put me here tonight but it will be useful, especially for Al, that I give background. Aunt Matty was more than an aunt to me, she was mother, aunt and best friend since my own mother died when I was five and Aunt Matty moved in to take care of me and my father. Although she was twenty-five years older, she was always friend above all else. It was she who taught me to garden, to survive in the wilderness, to build a kite and to fly it… the list goes on and on. Those of you who were at her Memorial Service will have heard me speak at considerable length about such things." She paused and flicked on the PowerPoint picture of Aunt Matty as well remembered from those early days.

"What you may not know is the final request which I received from her. A few days after her death, her executor came to my office and delivered a parcel. There was no mystery about its origin. I knew that handwriting as well as I know my own. Inside was a letter, some documents and a copy of her will." She hesitated for a moment and then put down her prepared remarks. "Look," she said, "if this is going to work, I need to be honest with you. I was angry with Aunt Matty when I read the letter with its plea, from beyond the grave, that I should take over here. She knew very well that I could scarcely say 'No,' but she seemed oblivious to the fact that I might find it almost impossible to do what she asked. She knew how little contact I had had, over the years, with the Church and I felt that I was being…" she hesitated, "… manipulated…" Her voice trailed off and there was a pause. Then Webster intervened with some reassurance: "Well, I guess we all understand how you must have felt. But in some ways, it's vintage Matty. She could always surprise us. Anyhow, I am glad you have agreed to do this. Matty always said that we learned together. Why don't we keep doing that."

There could scarcely have been a better way to move through the moment. It had been a bit awkward but old Webster had come through.

"All right," she said, "let's get on with it. Matthew's Gospel!" She took a deep breath.

"You will all be familiar with the fact that Matthew's Gospel is the first book of the New Testament," she began, hoping that she wasn't starting at too low a level. "I've been boning up on scholarly opinions and there seems to be some kind of consensus that Mark, the second Gospel, was written earlier. And that Matthew had access to it, or to some version of it."

Immediately, Al interrupted with a plea: "Remember people like me. This is all new and strange. Who was Matthew, anyhow and when was this thing written?" She could give an answer based on her reading but knew that every "fact" had given rise to dissent. "Al, it's a very good question," she said. "It's worth spending some time to recognize how little we really know. According to the Gospel account, Matthew was called away from his tax desk by Jesus. Just like that. Taxman one day, disciple of Jesus the next. So far, so good. But the authorship of the Gospel is anything but clear. Round about the year 125 A.D., someone called Papias wrote this, 'Matthew compiled the Sayings in Aramaic and everyone translated them as well as they could.' And that's about it. If I had to argue the case in court, I would be in big trouble. But we call it 'Matthew's Gospel' because we can't think of another way of discussing it. Maybe we should call it, 'the Gospel traditionally known as Matthew's'"

Al seemed disappointed with her answer but someone reminded the group that questions of date and authorship were not the main thing. "Let's encounter the text as if we received it as an anonymous writing. Maybe as an editor looking at an unsolicited manuscript."

That was the nudge forward, gratefully received. Melanie played on that theme. "What would an editor do with a manuscript that began like this?" she asked as she displayed the first section on the screen.

THE GENEALOGY OF JESUS CHRIST, THE SON OF DAVID, THE SON OF ABRAHAM

Abraham was the father of Isaac,

Isaac the father of Jacob,

and Jacob the father of Judah and his brothers.

Judah was the father of Perez and Zerah (by Tamar),

Perez was the father of Hezron,

Hezron the father of Ram,

Ram the father of Amminadab,

Amminadab the father of Nahshon,

Nahshon the father of Salmon

Salmon the father of Boaz (by Rahab)

Boaz the father of Obed (by Ruth)

Obed the father of Jesse

and Jesse the father of David the King.

David was the father of Solomon (by Uriah's wife)

Solomon was the father of Rehoboam,

Rehoboam was the father of Abijah,

Abijah was the father of Asa,

Asa was the father of Jehoshaphat,

Jehoshaphat was the father of Jehoram,

Jehoram was the father of Uzziah,

Uzziah was the father of Jotham,

Jotham was the father of Ahaz,

Ahaz was the father of Hezekiah,

Hezekiah was the father of Manasseh,

Manasseh was the father of Amon,

Amon was the father of Josiah

Josiah was the father of Jeconiah and his brothers at the time of the removal to Babylon

After the removal to Babylon, Jeconiah had a son Shealtiel

Shealtiel was the father of Zerubbabel

Zerubbabel was the father of Abiud

Abiud was the father of Eliakim

Eliakim was the father of Azor

Azor was the father of Zadok

Zadok was the father of Achim

Achim was the father of Eliud

Eliud was the father of Eleazar

Eleazar was the father of Matthan

Matthan was the father of Jacob

Jacob was the father of Joseph, the husband of Mary, who was the mother of Jesus who is called Christ

There are, therefore, in all, fourteen generations from Abraham to David; fourteen from David to the removal to Babylon; and fourteen from the removal to Babylon to the Christ.

Al took a close look at this and muttered, "Strewth! I didn't know that the Bible was like this!" Stephen, well known as a connoisseur of obscure information, needed to enlighten the group. "Did you know that 'strewth' is a mild expletive, popular in Australia. It had its origin in

'God's Truth', so maybe Al is onto something, eh!" This pedantic intervention was followed by another awkward pause.

Melanie pointed out that genealogies were now a huge cottage industry with all kinds of people excavating the roots of their family trees. But she agreed with Al that it was a rather intimidating beginning and recalled a day when she was snowed in and decided to have another attempt to read the New Testament. Unfortunately she chose the King James version with "the begats": "*Abraham begat Isaac, Isaac begat Jacob, and Jacob begat Judas and his brethren…*and on and on." She wondered how many people had been patient enough to go through all that and confessed that she had not.

She also commented that in the margin of Matty's copy of this text was a notation in French but that she would wait until they came back the next week to reveal it. "Otherwise, there won't be any drama in your lives." But the group was not so easily put off. "Come on, Melanie," they pleaded. "Matty didn't tease us like this!" So she relented and revealed that the words were, "cherchez les femmes". She urged them to read the genealogy with that injunction in mind. "Maybe your last message from Matty!"

This seemed to be a good place to end this first session, even though it was rather early. "You won't get off so lightly in future," she warned them. "When we get started on the text, we will be struggling to finish on time."

As she was walking across the parking lot, Al fell in step with her and she sensed that he had something to say. "I am a bit sorry that I used the word 'survivor' when I spoke at the beginning," he said. "Actually the experience was very positive. We even got a good meal together." Melanie remarked that they couldn't compete in the food direction. But Al had more to say. "Last year's group was extremely friendly. But there was a noticeable cooling when I told them I was gay." The conversation continued as she remarked that the church was still getting used to gay people, singles or couples. As he unlocked his bicycle from the rack, Al said, "I'm a single but looking out for Mr. Right." Melanie wondered why Al found it necessary to tell her all of this but she ended their conversation by saying, "I know the feeling. Let's hope that your Mr. Right isn't the same as mine!" And with that, they went their separate ways.

Chapter 1

Melanie was impressed that at 7.30 the next Tuesday evening, all were in their accustomed places, evidently ready for business. They seemed keen and eager to begin. "Here you are, all on time and ready. Aunt Matty trained you well!" She recalled to them a day when she had made a retreat in a monastery and had complimented a young monk about the punctuality of their services. "Well," he replied, "we are all creatures of habit."

She found it somehow pleasing that they stared at her for several seconds before letting loose with groaning. She had heard, long before, that this was their way of dealing with bad jokes.

She asked Webster for the opening prayer and he took the opportunity after the "Amen" to make a plug for his favorite aid to the study of the Gospels. He held up a well-worn volume. "Over the years, I have found it a great help to use this. It puts the three Gospels, Matthew, Mark and Luke, in parallel columns, arranged so that differences and similarities can be seen." Al asked, "What about John's Gospel?" and the answer seemed to satisfy him: that John's Gospel was so different from the other three that you could scarcely find any parallels with the others. Al said, "You might say that John's is an unparalleled Gospel!"

Pause, then the groans. Melanie remembered how Matty sometimes tried out her corny jokes on her before she left on Tuesday evenings. Another nostalgic moment.

But now, at last, they got down to the evening's work: the first chapter of Matthew. During the week, Melanie had asked Martha Henson, one of the group, to comment on Aunt Matty's direction: "Cherchez les femmes" She was a natural choice since she taught Women's Studies at the College.

She came well prepared and Melanie put up the genealogy on the screen again.

Martha cut to the chase: "This is a standard genealogy," she said, "except for the four women named: Tamar, Rahab, Ruth and Bathsheba. Without too much detail, here are thumbnail sketches:

Tamar was the resourceful widow who ensured the continuation of her husband's lineage by tricking her father-in-law, Judah, into having sex with her;

Rahab was a prostitute in Jericho who aided the invading Hebrews at the time of the conquest;

Ruth was a foreigner who married a wealthy kinsman of her deceased husband (and the text hints that she seduced him);

Bathsheba, wife of the honorable mercenary, Uriah, was taken adulterously by King David (after he arranged for Uriah's death)"

They all needed time to absorb this although, for most of them, this information was not unfamiliar as Matty had taken a previous study on "Women of the Bible." Al looked baffled, however. "I can see that I will have to do my homework. But from what Martha has said, I think that from now on I keep Bibles away from children!"

Webster had a more substantive comment. "I am surprised about your reference to Ruth. She has always been held up as a model of good behavior!" Martha agreed that the text of the book of Ruth in English translation was not so clear. "But the storyline has Ruth following her mother-in-law's instructions. 'She washed and perfumed herself and waited until Boaz was asleep. Then she approached quietly, uncovered his feet and lay down.' The Hebrew idiom for 'uncovering the feet' carries with it serious sexual overtones. And in Chapter 4, the elders of the village bless the happy couple with the words, 'May your family be like that of Perez, whom Tamar bore to Judah.'"

Melanie was concerned that the discussion, such as it was, had become too specialized. "Wow, we certainly dived in deep. And it's only Chapter 1," she said, partly to lighten the mood. She took the initiative to remind them all that background reading would be essential to get the most from these discussions and she put up the Bible references needed for Martha's list:

For Tamar, Genesis, Chapter 38
For Rahab, Joshua, Chapter 2
For Ruth, look between Judges and First Samuel
For Bathsheba, 2 Samuel, Chapter 11

She was impressed that most of them wrote it all down.

Martha then addressed their unspoken question: "Why make reference to these women and ignore all the others; Sarah, Rebecca and Rachel, wives of Abraham, Isaac and Jacob, for starters? It almost looks as if someone was trying to cast a cloud on the royal line, and in so doing, maligning David as well." There was some confused discussion. Someone thought that a later editor, with some malicious intent, might have inserted the names of the four women. Another wondered if it was because they were all probably non-Jewish, so that a hint was being given that the story to be told was the beginning of a new openness to Gentile people. Several thought that it was a preparation for the one who would be notorious for "eating and drinking with outcasts and sinners." But Martha had more to say. "What if we are looking at the four women in the wrong way? Whatever else we can say of them, it is clear that they were resourceful and determined ladies. One possibility: 'Matthew' was a woman!" Big silence. No one had thought of that and there was a resistance to the unfamiliar.

Melanie was pleased with all of this. It was opening lots of new ideas. "Let's keep Martha's suggestion in the back of our minds as we proceed. Maybe we'll find some other clues." Martha nodded. "I can make quite a case for female authorship," she insisted. "Wait for it!"

Melanie guided the conversation to the next big problem: why give a genealogy for Joseph when the text would immediately claim that Mary's pregnancy was of divine origin, so that Joseph wasn't the father at all? It was time to display the text of the second part of Chapter 1 and to wonder about the Virgin Birth.

> *The circumstances of the birth of Jesus Christ were these. After his mother Mary was betrothed to Joseph, before they were united in marriage, she was found to be with child through the Holy Spirit. But Joseph her husband, being a kind-hearted man and unwilling publicly to disgrace her, had determined to release her privately from the betrothal. But while he was contemplating this step, an angel of the Lord appeared to him in a dream and said, "Joseph, son of David, do not be afraid to bring home your wife Mary, for she is with child through the Holy Spirit. She will give birth to a son, and you are to call his name Jesus for he it is who will save his people from their sins." All this took place in fulfillment of what the Lord had spoken through the Prophet, "Behold! The virgin will be*

> with child and will give birth to a son, and they will call His name 'Immanuel' "—a word which signifies 'God with us'.
>
> When Joseph awoke, he did as the angel of the Lord had commanded, and brought home his wife, but did not live with her until she had given birth to a son. The child's name he called Jesus.

Someone asked if belief in that doctrine was essential. Creeds were quoted ("born of the Virgin Mary"). Stephen remarked that Paul, who wrote his letters before the Gospels were compiled, seemed unaware of such a belief, saying of Jesus only that he was "born of a woman". Al had been silent for a while and Melanie wondered if he was out of his depth. But he clearly had been doing his homework as he raised a question about the words of the prophet: "Behold! The virgin will be with child and will give birth to a son, and they will call His name Immanuel."

He said that he had read somewhere that the word "virgin" didn't appear in the original source and he wondered also why no one called Jesus "Immanuel". Martha, full of information, was quick to respond. "Al is right about the word 'virgin'. In the Hebrew text of Isaiah 7:14, where the quotation comes from, the word was "young woman." But when translation was made into Greek, the word for 'virgin' was used." Someone remembered the publication of the Revised Standard Version in 1952 when fundamentalist Christians attacked its translation of Isaiah 7:14 ("a young woman will conceive") as an undermining of the Doctrine of the Virgin Birth.

On the question of the name, "Immanuel," Webster remarked that it does not appear anywhere else in Matthew (or in any of the other Gospels, for that matter). Al added the comment: "We all hear 'Jesus Christ' used casually in the street. 'Immanuel Christ' would sound a little strange."

Webster had been looking ahead to Chapter 2 and he remarked that if one omitted the second part of Chapter 1, then the text flowed nicely and there would be no debate about Virgin Birth, which many Christians found problematic. They needed to look at the flow from the end of the genealogy:

> ... *Eliud was the father of Eleazar,*
> *Eleazar was the father of Matthan,*
> *Matthan was the father of Jacob,*

> *Jacob was the father of Joseph, the husband of Mary, who was the mother of Jesus who is called Christ*
>
> *There are, therefore, in all, fourteen generations from Abraham to David; fourteen from David to the Removal to Babylon; and fourteen from the Removal to Babylon to the Christ.*

And then go on to the beginning of Chapter 2:

> *Now after the birth of Jesus, which took place at Bethlehem in Judaea in the reign of King Herod, excitement was produced in Jerusalem by the arrival of certain Magi from the east, inquiring, "Where is the newly born king of the Jews? For we have seen his Star in the east, and have come here to do him homage."*

Since Chapter 2 was the topic for the following week, Melanie displayed the full text for all to ponder:

> *Now after the birth of Jesus, which took place at Bethlehem in Judaea in the reign of King Herod, excitement was produced in Jerusalem by the arrival of certain Magi from the east, inquiring, "Where is the newly born king of the Jews? For we have seen his Star in the east, and have come here to do him homage." Reports of this soon reached the king, and greatly agitated not only him but all the people of Jerusalem. So he assembled all the High Priests and Scribes of the people, and anxiously asked them where the Christ was to be born.*
>
> *"At Bethlehem in Judaea," they replied; "for so it stands written in the words of the Prophet, 'And thou, Bethlehem in the land of Judah, by no means the least honorable among princely places in Judah! For from thee shall come a prince—one who shall be the Shepherd of My People Israel.'"*
>
> *Thereupon Herod sent privately for the Magi and ascertained from them the exact time of the star's appearing. He then directed them to go to Bethlehem, adding, "Go and make careful inquiry about the child, and when you have found him, bring me word, that I too may come and do him homage." After hearing what the king said, they went to Bethlehem, while, strange to say, the star they had seen in the east led them on until it came and stood over the place where the babe was. When they saw the star, the sight filled them with intense joy. So they entered the house; and when*

they saw the babe with his mother Mary, they prostrated themselves and did him homage, and opening their treasure-chests offered gifts to him—gold, frankincense, and myrrh. But being forbidden by God in a dream to return to Herod, they went back to their own country by a different route.

When they were gone, an angel of the Lord appeared to Joseph in a dream and said, "Rise: take the babe and His mother and escape to Egypt, and remain there till I bring you word. For Herod is about to make search for the child in order to destroy him."

So Joseph roused himself and took the babe and his mother by night and departed into Egypt. There he remained till Herod's death, that what the Lord had said through the Prophet might be fulfilled, "Out of Egypt I called My Son."

Then Herod, finding that the Magi had trifled with him, was furious, and sent and massacred all the boys under two years of age, in Bethlehem and all its neighborhood, according to the date he had so carefully ascertained from the Magi. Then were these words, spoken by the Prophet Jeremiah, fulfilled,

"A voice was heard in Ramah, wailing and bitter lamentation: it was Rachel bewailing her children, and she refused to be comforted because they were no more."

But after Herod's death, an angel of the Lord appeared in a dream to Joseph in Egypt, and said to him, "Rise from sleep, and take the child and His mother, and go into the land of Israel, for those who were seeking the child's life are dead." So he roused himself and took the child and His mother and came into the land of Israel. But hearing that Archelaus had succeeded his father Herod on the throne of Judaea, he was afraid to go there; and being instructed by God in a dream he withdrew into Galilee, and went and settled in a town called Nazareth, in order that these words spoken through the Prophets might be fulfilled, "He shall be called a Nazarene."

They read the familiar words and thought about Webster's suggestion that the Virgin Birth narrative might have been a later addition to the text. "It almost looks as though some one slipped in an extra page and didn't change anything else." This gave rise to a debate about such a possibility. "Surely you wouldn't get away with tampering with Holy Writ." It was pointed out that in the early times, the writing wouldn't have such stature and it could be done and copies of the new text circulated. They were now getting used to the idea that their discussions were going to be often inconclusive. As Webster said, "I am putting forward this idea but don't have any evidence for it, so I will go on saying the Creed every Sunday!"

A new contribution was made by Andrew who had, up to this point, joined in the general discussion without saying anything particularly memorable. Andrew was a considerable reader of Bishop Spong, the controversial bishop of the Episcopal Church of the U.S.A. He wished to acquaint the group with the idea of *midrash*, a way of interpreting a text which had been developed by Jewish rabbis: to take a text and "fill in the details," as he put it, using careful imagination. "Spong is entranced with the idea that midrashic interpretation is the key to understanding the Gospels," Andrew reported. "He thinks that Matthew Chapter 2 is a midrash on Old Testament texts." The argument went something like this: early Christians, still thinking of themselves as a part of Judaism, trawled the Jewish scriptures for predictions which might apply to their Leader. The four which are quoted in Matthew, Chapter 2, then provided a framework for imaginative story telling; since Jesus was the fulfillment of all these texts, his life must have been thus and so. It is then possible to build the midrash and get Chapter 2 as we have it today.

This line of thought was hotly contested in the group, with a majority finding it hard to believe that anyone could "get away with it."

Melanie sensed that the evening had been rather successful and that her time as leader would have its moments. The group seemed inclined to continue after the appointed hour but she dismissed them and heard the discussions continuing as they left the room. She was about to leave when Webster, who had lingered behind the others, asked for "a quick word." They sat down again and he began. "Melanie, things are going so well but I feel the need to apologize," he said. "I am saying too much and I want you to keep me in check. Matty was good at that."

Melanie smiled, partly with relief. She thought that perhaps she was going to hear something negative about her leadership. "Dear Webster," she said. "You are so full of enthusiasm and when you spoke tonight, I watched the faces around the table. They were eating it up." She paused and they exchanged affectionate glances before they, too, went on their way.

Chapter 2

It seemed only a short time before they were back at it again. They had all had time to re-read Chapter 2 and Melanie displayed the first part of the text on the screen.

> Now after the birth of Jesus, which took place at Bethlehem in Judaea in the reign of King Herod, excitement was produced in Jerusalem by the arrival of certain Magi from the east, inquiring, "Where is the newly born king of the Jews? For we have seen his Star in the east, and have come here to do him homage." Reports of this soon reached the king, and greatly agitated not only him but all the people of Jerusalem. So he assembled all the High Priests and Scribes of the people, and anxiously asked them where the Christ was to be born.
>
> "At Bethlehem in Judaea," they replied; "for so it stands written in the words of the Prophet, 'And thou, Bethlehem in the land of Judah, by no means the least honorable among princely places in Judah! For from thee shall come a prince—one who shall be the Shepherd of my people Israel.'"
>
> Thereupon Herod sent privately for the Magi and ascertained from them the exact time of the star's appearing. He then directed them to go to Bethlehem, adding, "Go and make careful inquiry about the child, and when you have found him, bring me word, that I too may come and do him homage." After hearing what the king said, they went to Bethlehem, while, strange to say, the star they had seen in the east led them on until it came and stood over the place where the babe was. When they saw the star, the sight filled them with intense joy. So they entered the house; and when they saw the babe with his mother Mary, they prostrated themselves and did him homage, and opening their treasure-chests offered gifts to him—gold, frankincense, and myrrh. But being

forbidden by God in a dream to return to Herod, they went back to their own country by a different route.

"I suppose," she said, "that this is the best known part of the whole Gospel. When we raise questions about its historicity, we'll feel a bit like the Grinch who stole Christmas. But I have been thinking this week about Andrew's comments on 'midrash', an idea that was completely new to me." Andrew replied, "It isn't so strange. After all it's what preachers do to Biblical texts, filling in the details from their imagination. Sometimes they do it well, but not always." Melanie confessed that she had steered clear of sermons most of her life!

Someone wondered why the full quote about Bethlehem wasn't given since the original in Micah 5 goes on ". . . out of you will come a ruler . . . whose origins . . . are from days of eternity."

There was some discussion about Magi, with Stephen recounting his childhood memory of being a sheep in the Christmas pageant, hoping one day to be a shepherd and seeing the Magi as almost divine. Melanie recalled the Menotti opera, *Amahl and the Night Visitors*. They were not all familiar with this piece so she explained that it had been a commissioned work and that the composer, Gian Carlo Menotti, had drawn inspiration from the Bosch masterpiece *The Adoration of the Magi* which he had seen in the New York Metropolitan Museum of Art. She outlined the plot: the Magi seek shelter in the hut of a poor widow whose crippled son, enchanted by the quest, offers to donate his crutch to the newborn, and thereby receives healing.

"Do you see?" said Andrew, more animated than they had ever seen him. "It's a midrash on Matthew's Magi text. A midrash on a midrash!" Al went even further. "It's more," he said. "It begins with Matthew's text, then Bosch makes a visual midrash and Menotti makes a musical one on that!"

Webster moved the discussion along by reminding them that the "other half" of the Christmas story is in Luke's Gospel with the census, "no room at the inn," the shepherds and the angels. "Does it matter," he wondered, "that we might have some doubts about the details, whether they actually happened that way? Perhaps it's enough to enter into the story. After all, when we go to a performance of *Hamlet*, we don't worry too much about historical origins of the story, even though there was probably a seventh century Danish prince of that name. And no one has dug up Elsinore to find his castle. We just enter into the story." Then Al took that argument to its logical conclusion. "How would we feel if the whole Gospel was viewed in the same way? Could we 'just enter into the story'?" There was a considerable pause; some were shocked at this idea but all were challenged by it.

Again, it was time to move along:

> When they were gone, an angel of the Lord appeared to Joseph in a dream and said, "Rise: take the babe and his mother and escape to Egypt, and remain there till I bring you word. For Herod is about to make search for the child in order to destroy him." So Joseph roused himself and took the babe and his mother by night and departed into Egypt. There he remained till Herod's death, that what the Lord had said through the Prophet might be fulfilled, "Out of Egypt I called My Son."
>
> Then Herod, finding that the Magi had trifled with him, was furious, and sent and massacred all the boys under two years of age, in Bethlehem and all its neighborhood, according to the date he had so carefully ascertained from the Magi. Then were these words, spoken by the Prophet Jeremiah, fulfilled, "A voice was heard in Ramah, wailing and bitter lamentation: It was Rachel bewailing her children, and she refused to be comforted because there were no more."
>
> But after Herod's death, an angel of the Lord appeared in a dream to Joseph in Egypt, and said to him, "Rise from sleep, and take the child and his mother, and go into the land of Israel, for those who were seeking the child's life are dead." So he roused himself and took the child and his mother and came into the land of Israel. But hearing that Archelaus had succeeded his father Herod on the throne of Judaea, he was afraid to go there; and being instructed by God in a dream he withdrew into Galilee, and went and settled in a town called Nazareth, in order that these words spoken through the Prophets might be fulfilled, "He shall be called a Nazarene."

She asked them to notice how frequently the events were said to be "so that the prophecy would be fulfilled": Bethlehem as birthplace, Rachel weeping for her children as a predictor of Herod's massacre, the flight into Egypt so that the "out of Egypt have I called my son" and the residence in Nazareth so that "he will be called a Nazarene." She remarked, "I understand that no-one has found any source for the Nazarene prophecy. Perhaps it's from a book that didn't make it into the canon." There was some argument about the relation between the predictions and their fulfillments. Stephen thought that the idea of taking refuge in Egypt was a bit far fetched. "Why not just go to another village? Or to Nazareth? And the 'out of Egypt, I called my son' in its original context referred to the Exodus, surely, without any larger meaning." They agreed, reluctantly, that if it were Midrash, it wasn't so skillfully done.

Stephen wanted to go back to the star. He wondered, for starters, how a star could lead anyone except in a general direction. Any star directly overhead at Bethlehem will be directly overhead any other village in Judaea. Some looked a bit puzzled and he explained that stars were so far away that moving yourself a few miles didn't change a star's direction in any measurable way. Melanie needed to nudge him along. "There is a long history of people trying to identify the star of Bethlehem," she said. "Newspapers publish, rather breathlessly, each December, the latest 'discoveries'; sometimes a conjunction of planets, sometimes a meteor or, more recently, a supernova. It makes better sense to accept the ancient tradition that when a great person is born, there are signs in heaven to confirm the event." But Stephen wouldn't be denied. Evidently he had been doing his homework, for he quoted from the Book of Numbers, chapter 24, the text, "A star will come out of Jacob and a scepter will rise out of Israel." He wondered why the author of Matthew didn't quote this verse.

There was a feeling of restlessness, as often was the case when Stephen held the floor, partly because of his style but, on this occasion, because no-one could think of anything sensible to say. And while this didn't always bring proceedings to an end, on this occasion, it did.

As she drove home, Melanie felt discontent with the evening; so much had been passed over so quickly. She had been hoping that someone would want to talk about the dreams mentioned in the text. So many dreams in the first two chapters and then only one more in the whole gospel: to the wife of Pilate. She wondered idly if Jesus ever dreamed. "Maybe the Kingdom is his dream." Her rambling thoughts distracted her and before she knew it, she had missed her turn off the highway. Her way home would pass through unfamiliar parts of town but eventually she drew up, relieved, into her parking place. It had been another memorable evening.

Chapter 3

A SMALL COFFEE SHOP near the Cathedral was a favorite hangout for locals and on the following Monday morning at about 10, Melanie, Al, and Webster had taken over one of its more remote tables for a discussion of progress to date.

She wanted their candid opinions and wasn't disappointed; the two of them had obviously been in touch and had agreed that things were going well. They both acknowledged that, without serious commitment to "homework," the Tuesday gatherings would be too much, too fast. Matthew's Gospel had twenty-eight chapters and it was going to be a scramble to get through in one year. Melanie said, "It's like being in a straight jacket. I am dreading the Sermon on the Mount chapters. It's almost impossible to do justice to all that stuff!" But the other two thought it would be better to keep the chapter a week schedule. "Leave us something to read at home," suggested Webster.

"Part of my trouble," she grumbled, "is my idea that we should do more rather than less. For example, what about looking at the 1964 movie on Matthew's Gospel by Pasolini? You might not know," she said, addressing Al, "that I am a bit of a movie buff and have a copy at home. It's black and white and takes a very literal approach but it has a power of a very special kind. But that would take a whole evening." Webster replied, "If you want ideas along that line, I have a friend who teaches New Testament. He visits me occasionally and would probably be willing to come along and tell us what's going on out there in the world of the scholars."

In the end they agreed to keep going as best they could and Al suggested that Melanie would need to keep talkers like him "under control."

Their conversation came to no clear conclusions but it was brought to an end when Al, indicating that he was about to depart, stood and raised his glass of Sprite, toasting their joint enterprise with the words,

"I drink to your well-being!" before leaving to take his bicycle from the rack outside. Webster and Melanie exchanged glances. "Are you thinking what I'm thinking," she said, "that we have a jester on our hands?" Webster grinned at her. "Indeed, it does occur to me that a sprite is a kind of water spirit, often associated with wells!" he said. "Watch out for Al's sense of humor."

Back in business the next evening, the group agreed that they had read Chapter 3 in advance so that the overhead was just a reminder. Several commented that the text displayed was not quite the same as what they had read. Melanie explained, "Aunt Matty was rather partial to the Weymouth Translation of 1903 because there was some family connection to Richard Weymouth. Since the overheads were already prepared, I have gone along with them and made a few alterations here and there when I think that Weymouth is a bit obscure!"

They looked impressed and she hastened to assure them that she was not a Greek scholar but had tried simply to smooth out the English.

So there it was:

> About this time John the Baptist made his appearance, preaching in the desert of Judaea. "Repent," he said, "for the Kingdom of Heaven is now close at hand."
>
> He it is who was spoken of through the Prophet Isaiah when he said, "The voice of one crying aloud, 'In the desert prepare a road for the Lord: make His highway straight.'"
>
> This man John wore a garment of camel's hair, and a loincloth of leather; and he lived upon locusts and wild honey. Then large numbers of people went out to him—people from Jerusalem and from all Judaea, and from the whole of the Jordan valley— and were baptized by him in the Jordan, making full confession of their sins.
>
> But when he saw many of the Pharisees and Sadducees coming for baptism, he exclaimed, "O vipers' brood, who has warned you to flee from the coming wrath? Therefore let your lives prove your change of heart; and do not imagine that you can say to yourselves, 'We have Abraham as our forefather,' for I tell you that God can raise up descendants for Abraham from these stones. And already the axe is lying at the root of the trees, so that every tree which does not produce good fruit will quickly be hewn down and thrown into the fire.

I indeed am baptizing you in water on a profession of repentance; but He who is coming after me is mightier than I: His sandals I am not worthy to carry for a moment; He will baptize you in the Holy Spirit and in fire. His winnowing-shovel is in His hand, and He will make a thorough clearance of His threshing-floor, gathering His wheat into the storehouse, but burning up the chaff in unquenchable fire."

Just at that time Jesus, coming from Galilee to the Jordan, presented himself to John to be baptized by him. John protested. "It is I," he said, "who have need to be baptized by you, and do you come to me?"

"Let it be so on this occasion," Jesus replied; "for so we ought to fulfil every religious duty." Then he consented; and Jesus was baptized, and immediately went up from the water. At that moment the heavens opened, and he saw the Spirit of God descending like a dove and alighting upon Him, while a voice came from Heaven, saying, "This is My Son, the dearly loved, in whom is My delight."

They were all ready for discussion: Stephen couldn't wait to tell anyone who would listen about the persistence of the John the Baptist loyalists into the next generation, that in Acts 19, Paul arrives in Ephesus and finds disciples of John the Baptist alive and well there. And Webster had a handout ready to be distributed, showing a page from his "Gospel Parallels" in which the various accounts of John the Baptist were put side by side. Then, someone wanted to know how bad the Pharisees and Sadducees were, really, that they were singled out for such condemnation; maybe they were truly interested in what John had to say . . . and what about all the threats of fire?

For the first time, Melanie was perplexed. It wasn't the start she had envisioned. There was energy in the group but the possibility of anarchy. So she called them to order and appealed for a more systematic approach to the text. "Let's start at the beginning; there's safety in that!"

Putting aside her discomfiture, she tried an introduction:

"For this chapter, then, we have high drama; this wild man from the desert (according to Luke, a cousin of Jesus) and his fiery rhetoric. Even his first recorded words might get him into trouble as talk of 'the Kingdom' would play into popular expectations of liberation from Roman rule. And his scathing denunciations of the Pharisees and

Sadducees made sure of their enmity." She paused and looked around the group, realizing that she was in full lecture mode, exactly what she had vowed to avoid. "Did anyone have better luck than I," she asked, " in discovering why John came on so hot and heavy?"

Some thought that it was a reflection of later conflicts between the early church and the ascendant Pharisaic influence in Judaism in the later part of the first century. But against that idea was the fact that Sadducees had disappeared by the year 70 so their inclusion as enemies would be somewhat redundant. Several had read up on the Pharisees and identified them as pious Jews, keen to keep the law in every detail. They wondered if the scrupulous observance of purity laws by Pharisees was an effective barrier to all but the leisured classes and that they thereby created a barrier to "the outcasts and sinners" with whom Jesus had such sympathy. "If you're a working man, grabbing lunch from a street vendor, there isn't much time and place for handwashing!"

It was then time to think about baptism, especially the baptism of Jesus and the awkward moment when John is portrayed as acknowledging his own need. The reply of Jesus" . . . we must fulfill every religious duty," was identified as a strange explanation since earlier the baptism was accompanied by confession of sins.

Webster recalled having read debates about that text within the church from the beginning, finding uneasiness in the idea of Jesus as needing to repent or to confess sins. He tried again one of his hypotheses: "I understand 'repentance' to mean a change of life's direction, so it isn't too difficult to see Jesus at a turning point. Maybe with a new awareness of his destiny as preacher of the Kingdom." "So far, so good," Andrew said, "I guess that I can buy that but what about 'sin'. The church has always claimed Jesus to be sinless. There seems to be the options: either give up that teaching and see Jesus as a sinner like the rest of us. Or find some other meaning for his baptism." There were nods around the table and an eagerness to see if Webster could stick handle his way around this. "Well," he began, "I agree it's a bit tricky. My feeling is that we define 'sin' a bit too narrowly. The actual word carries the connotation of 'missing the mark'. Maybe Jesus saw his thirty years up to that moment as somehow spent in avoiding his destiny."

"It's quite a big 'maybe'" replied Andrew "But it's certainly worth some thought." And Melanie rounded off their exchange by expressing gratitude that "here is a safe place to be creative!"

Finally, the familiar episode of the dove, the voice and the commendation. Was this observed by all? Or did Jesus speak later (to his disciples?) of some mystical experience at his baptism? Melanie raised these issues and she was surprised when Stephen, whose interventions to date had been rather irritating, spoke quite movingly of his own experience as a teenage boy, being baptized in a river in Manitoba and the lasting impression made by that event. He confided that each year on August 10, he celebrated the anniversary of his baptism by attending a Eucharist wherever he might be and renewing his baptismal vows. All present were impressed and rather surprised; Al, who had been silent most of the evening, acknowledged that he had never been baptized and thanked Stephen in a very cordial manner for his sharing.

As the time for ending the session came closer, Al suddenly came up with a suggestion which took Melanie quite by surprise. "Leading a group like this is not easy," he said, "and we know that Melanie didn't exactly volunteer for the job. Why don't we take turns at introducing the chapter and then go on from there?" Melanie felt her anger rising but she kept herself as calm as she could. "Why," she wondered to herself, "hadn't Al had the courtesy to raise the matter in their coffee shop conversation?" She was somewhat mollified as Al continued. "Melanie," he said, "don't take this as a criticism. It's just an idea which occurred to me this minute." She had come to realize that Matty had held the group in control by the force of her personality and that she wasn't in the same league. She decided that two could play at the game of surprises. "Actually, it would suit me quite well to have someone else take over next week. There's a lot going on at the office. And since you raised this, Al, what about taking it on?" She was a bit startled when he agreed.

They went their separate ways, somewhat surprised by the turn of events. Al tried his best to continue his reassurances in the parking lot and Melanie felt that she should be magnanimous. "Al, we will be looking forward to next week," was her parting remark

Chapter 4

Al could devote time the following week to some sober second thoughts. His agreement to give an introduction to the next chapter of Matthew had been impulsive. It wasn't that he shrank from the task, exactly, but rather that he wanted to avoid giving a lecture and then waiting for questions. There was also the little matter of being a complete newcomer to Bible reading! He remained uneasy and regretful about his impulsive action, hoping that his relationship with Melanie wouldn't be soured by his suggestion.

He sighed as he sat at his desk in the bookstore. It was a familiar location where he was well able to keep an eye on comings and goings. There was George, one of the regulars, a collector of Victorian children's books, browsing but rarely making a purchase. And Brian, shabby and sad, finding the bookstore a warm, dry place. He occasionally surprised Al by his knowledge of books but had never yet bought one.

He knew them well and left them alone.

He called up the first part of the text onto his screen and examined it closely.

> *At that time Jesus was led up by the Spirit into the desert in order to be tempted by the Devil. There he fasted for forty days and nights; and after that he suffered from hunger. So the Tempter came and said, "If you are the Son of God, command these stones to turn into loaves."*
>
> *"It is written," replied Jesus, "It is not on bread alone that a man shall live, but on whatsoever God shall appoint."*
>
> *Then the Devil took him to the Holy City and caused him to stand on the roof of the Temple, and said, "If you are God's Son, throw yourself down; for it is written, 'To His angels He will give orders concerning thee, and on their hands they shall bear thee up, lest at any moment thou shouldst strike thy foot against a stone.'"*

> "Again it is written," replied Jesus, 'Thou shalt not put the Lord thy God to the proof.'"
>
> Then the Devil took him to the top of an exceedingly lofty mountain, from which he caused him to see all the Kingdoms of the world and their splendour, and said to him, "All this I will give you, if you will kneel down and do me homage."
>
> "Begone, Satan!" Jesus replied; "for it is written, 'To the Lord thy God thou shalt do homage, and to Him alone shalt thou render worship'." Thereupon the Devil left him, and angels at once came and ministered to him.

Firstly, then, the Temptation story with Jesus off in the desert, the forty days and nights of fasting and the three-fold testing. He guessed that the Temptation narrative might provoke lots of discussion. He glanced at the other parts of the chapter. They seemed to be the account of picking up where John the Baptist left off, finding disciples and beginning an itinerant ministry in which proclamation was augmented by powerful deeds.

He checked out the Temptation story and became aware that it fell into a well-known category; he reread parts of Joseph Campbell's "Hero with a Thousand Faces" and recognized the temptation narrative as an account of a series of ordeals that Jesus had to face on his journey. The puzzle was making sense of the conversation; when the suggestion comes that he should make bread from stones, his reply seems a non-sequitur. No one is suggesting that men should live by bread alone but simply that he should satisfy his own hunger. Al thought about a reference to "fast food" as a kind of joke but thought better of it.

The temptation to create a sensational miracle is countered by the general notion that one should not put God to the test. The last of the three seemed simply bizarre at first glance: who in their right mind would entertain the notion of becoming a servant of Satan for the sake of political power? He paused a bit over that thought, reminding himself of those in the history of mankind who had seemingly done just that!

Was it possible, he wondered, that Jesus gave his followers a general description of his time in the desert and that later writers did the Midrash thing again, complete with citations from the Jewish scriptures? It would certainly explain the dialogue, which, he thought, was somewhat lame;

surely Jesus and his opponent could debate more profoundly than the record seemed to indicate.

He wondered again if it was possible to penetrate the mind of Jesus. Could it have been the case that he was unaware of his destiny until he was baptized and experienced the events around his baptism, then needed to get away into the desert to try to sort it out? Could he have eventually shared with his disciples something of the struggles to answer the question, "If I am the Messiah, what should I do to fulfil that destiny?" The three temptations might conceal underlying options: to provide bread for the people as a benefactor, to make some spectacular manifestation of his Messianic powers, to find political action to inaugurate the Kingdom.

His mind drifted inevitably to his memory of "The Last Temptation of Christ," both the book which he had read in his teenage years when he had first fallen in love with the writings of Nikos Kazantzakis, and the more recent movie. He wondered again if the "Last Temptation," to avoid the messianic destiny and to live a "normal" life, might in fact be the "First Temptation". He remembered the parable in "Report to Greco," wondering if he could include it in his presentation. He was too lazy to look it up but recalled the story line: Mary and Joseph bring their son, Jesus, to a sage in Jerusalem. Mary cries out that her son needs healing. In private conversation, the sage asks the boy the source of his trouble. He confesses to great pain and restlessness; "I roam the streets, wrestling," he says. To the question, "Wrestling with whom?" comes the reply, "With God, of course! Who else?" For a month, the boy receives treatment, herbs, quietness and reassurance. After that time, he is cured. He goes back to Galilee to become "the best carpenter in Nazareth." The parable ends with the sage saying, "Do you understand? Jesus was cured. Instead of saving the world, he became the best carpenter in Nazareth!"

He thought about this story again, as he had over the years, unsure that it would fit into the discussion, but moved again by its power.

Regretfully, he recognized that he was wandering away from Matthew's text.

He was interrupted for a while by the needs of business and thoughts of Melanie, as he hoped again that he hadn't given the impression that he wished to take over leadership of the group. His initial ponderings on the temptation narrative made him realize what a difficult situation she had been inherited.

At that very time, Melanie was meeting with the Dean of the Cathedral, ostensibly on some legal business but she was glad of the opportunity that the meeting gave to discuss her "inheritance" from Matty. "Yes," he agreed, "it came as a bit of a surprise when I heard about it. But I have confidence that you will find your way through it. Is it Matty's last attempt to bring you into the fold?" He laughed and she couldn't help lightening up a bit. "But," she said, "there is another problem." And she explained her exchange with Al and his agreement to make an introduction the following Tuesday. "He's totally new to it all. It is possibly the first time he has read Matthew's Gospel."

"Don't worry," he replied. "I know Al quite well from his bookstore and he is an interesting man. And think what a rare opportunity to get a take on a gospel chapter from an outsider perspective."

Al had time later that day to return to the remainder of the text; it seemed less problematic.

> Now when Jesus heard that John was thrown into prison, he withdrew into Galilee, and, leaving Nazareth, he went and settled at Capernaum, a town by the Lake on the frontiers of Zebulun and Naphtali, in order that these words, spoken through the Prophet Isaiah, might be fulfilled,
>
> "Zebulun's land and Naphtali's land; the road by the Lake; the country beyond the Jordan; Galilee of the Nations!
>
> The people who were dwelling in darkness have seen a brilliant light; and on those who were dwelling in the region of the shadow of death, on them light has dawned."

It made sense that when John the Baptist was no longer able to continue, that Jesus would take over, with identically the same description of his preaching, *Repent for the Kingdom of Heaven is now close at hand.*

The circumstances of John's imprisonment were easily tracked down in Matthew 14, with the gruesome account of his beheading to satisfy the malice of Herodias. He remembered being present for a production of Strauss's opera at the Sydney Opera House, unprepared for the shocking ending when Salome herself is beheaded at Herod's command. His mind had wandered away again from the text and he knew that Strauss was too far removed from Matthew's Gospel to be of significance to the task in hand.

But a question which came naturally: if Jesus inherits John's proclamation, did he also continue the baptisms? A quick web check made it clear that this was a debating point: John's Gospel goes to some trouble to say that ". . . in fact it was not Jesus who baptized but his disciples" (John 4.2). Yet earlier (John 3.22) it is stated that ". . . Jesus and his disciples went out into the Judaean countryside where he spent some time with them and baptized." Al wondered if that meant that Jesus baptized his disciples and then turned baptizing over to them?

The calling of the first four disciples seemed straightforward.

> *From that time Jesus began to preach. "Repent," he said, "for the Kingdom of Heaven is now close at hand."*
>
> *And walking along the shore of the Lake of Galilee he saw two brothers—Simon called Peter and his brother Andrew—throwing a dragnet into the Lake; for they were fishers. And he said to them, "Come and follow me, and I will make you fishers of men." So they immediately left their nets and followed him. As he went further on, he saw two other brothers, James the son of Zebedee and his brother John, in the boat with their father Zebedee mending their nets; and he called them. And they at once left the boat and their father, and followed him.*

Had they been disciples of John the Baptist, he wondered. If so, it would make sense that they might give allegiance to the one who had received the accolade, "He who is coming after me is mightier than I." He felt that he was generally in touch with the chapter but remained apprehensive about guiding the discussion.

Tuesday came quickly enough and Al sat uneasily in his accustomed chair, waiting for Melanie to call upon him. He felt a little like a schoolboy waiting for the teacher to call him up for an oral presentation.

Things began well enough as Melanie obligingly put up the Temptation narrative on the screen.

He began: "This week, I read Matthew Chapter 4 for the very first time! I tried to put myself in the place of one of the early listeners, maybe in the first century, who was in an equivalent situation." He looked around, relieved that they seemed to be paying close attention. "All of you, I guess, have heard many sermons on the Temptation in the Wilderness. But I am starting from scratch. It was Andrew who introduced me to the idea of Midrash last week and that got me thinking.

Maybe Jesus shared with his disciples the general outlines of his experiences in the desert and then a later generation filled in the details, using texts from the Jewish scriptures."

"Does it make sense," he wondered, "to see the baptism and the temptation as a continuous narrative? Jesus experiences something special at his baptism, becomes aware of the possibility that he is The One and goes off into solitude to try to sort it out. The three 'temptations' might represent options in the fulfillment of his destiny."

He left it to the general discussion that followed to sort out meanings for the temptations, especially with reference to modern life. Martha Henson, in particular, saw possible parallels in the life of the Church. She spoke at some length. "I wonder if the turning stones into bread might represent social action, good in itself but scarcely 'every word from the mouth of God' as my translation puts it. And maybe the Temple temptation is parallel to the need for extravagant display." She paused, seeming to lose confidence. "And the temptation to find an alliance with secular power is only too well a part of the church's history."

She conceded that she had heard a sermon along these lines and there was some discussion with the consensus, tactfully expressed within the group, that it was all a bit far fetched. Al was impressed with the way that Melanie tried to build on Martha's idea. "What if Jesus, at that stage, saw himself simply as the new leader of John the Baptist's disciples? Then maybe the temptations might relate to perils of leadership. I haven't thought out the details but I think it can work." Martha became quite animated. "Yes," she replied. "It is a better fit. Any leader might indeed be tempted to look after his own needs, to draw too much attention to himself or to form an alliance with the 'Dark Side'!"

Al decided to move the discussion along, giving his own thoughts about the temptations as possible approaches to the fulfillment of the messianic destiny; Jesus, hungry and exhausted in the desert, thinking, "If I am the Messiah, how do I now proceed?" This was a cue that they, at least, needed to proceed!

Al wondered about the imprisonment of John the Baptist. "It's mentioned here but then introduced much later in the Gospel as a new event. I know we shouldn't look forward into later chapters but Matthew 14 gives the whole story. Why John was imprisoned and the horrors of his death. It's as though Matthew needed a good editor."

He would have passed over the reference to Jesus moving his place of residence from Nazareth to Capernaum. But Webster's intervened: "Here's where the Gospel Parallels are useful. If I look across to Luke's account of this event, I see that it is the result of a dramatic episode. Jesus preaches in his hometown synagogue and infuriates his people by reference to stories in which Gentiles, the widow from Sidon and the foreign general Naaman from Syria, received the benefits of miraculous intervention." He went on to read the text from Luke 4:

> *"When they heard this, all in the synagogue were filled with wrath. And they rose up and put him out of the city and led him to the brow of the hill on which their city was built that they might throw him down headlong. But passing through their midst, he went away, down to the city of Capernaum."*

"A simple statement of fact in Matthew conceals a great deal," he concluded.

Al was rather taken by surprise. "I see what you meant when you spoke last week about Gospel Parallels. Matthew says he moved house in order to fulfil the prophecy of Isaiah but one could argue from Luke's Gospel that he went away because Nazareth was too hot to hold him!" And, to clinch the point, Webster reported that he had made a check of references to Nazareth and found that nothing is said about Jesus ever visiting it again.

So to the next section: Al began by observing that it would be natural for Jesus to continue John's preaching. "I spent a bit of time on the question of whether Jesus baptized anyone." He outlined his findings and was disappointed that no one responded. And indeed he realized that he had strayed away from the text. He was now feeling that things hadn't gone well and he looked over to Melanie, who had been silent for most of the evening, for rescue.

She was ready to take over the reins. "Thanks, Al. You've given us plenty to think about. But the big question remains: what did Jesus mean by the Kingdom of Heaven?" She paused to let that sink in. Then she continued. "In the package which I received from Aunt Matty, there was a copy of a book by the American biblical scholar, Norman Perrin. It's called 'The Kingdom of God in the Teaching of Jesus' and it tells me more than I want to know on the subject." She paused and tried to relax. "Perrin's book shows that the scholars agree that 'The Kingdom of

Heaven' in Matthew's Gospel and 'The Kingdom of God' in Mark and Luke can be regarded as meaning exactly the same thing and that the term 'Kingdom' means the 'reign of God' rather than a physical area. It would seem, however, that everything else is disputed. One of the main issues is whether the Kingdom is present in the new community being formed around Jesus or whether it is something yet to come, and to come with an overthrow of the world's powers by God's intervention. Or somehow, that both can be true!"

She paused again, realizing that she had little more to contribute. "Let's put such questions to one side and check them out as we continue though Matthew. Right now, I am looking at the clock and thinking about next week."

Al said, "I want to thank Melanie for her graciousness. I made a foolish offer last week and have had the whole week to regret it. I'm not eager to do it again." No one else showed any keenness to substitute as leader and Melanie said, "Just when I was thinking I was off the hook . . . But get ready to roll up your sleeves. The next three weeks will be devoted to the Sermon on the Mount. Lots to talk about."

They went off, continuing the discussion in the parking lot. And she went off, feeling pleased that calm had been restored.

Chapter 5

That night, Melanie lay awake for some time. She realized that she had used the reference to Perrin's book and her little exposition about the Kingdom of God partly to show Al that she was in charge. Perrin's book, which she had only skimmed, reminded her that she could easily get into deep water. She felt like someone overhearing a conversation which had been going on for hours and trying to participate. Except that in this case the conversation had been going on for generations. Aunt Matty's choice to include such a book in the package was not helpful. She wondered if Matty had read it. There were no signs of her characteristic underlinings. Worse yet, there was no escaping from further discussions of the Kingdom of Heaven. She had a count of more than fifty references in the remainder of the Gospel. And she had realized, too late, that she had cut off the discussion of the calling of the first disciples and the summary of the powerful actions of Jesus at the end of the chapter.

Eventually she drifted off to sleep, glad that the morrow would present her with legal matters on which she felt she was on firm ground.

Throughout the week, she read the text for the next meeting with some care. Keeping a respectful distance from any expert opinion, she could see that what was commonly called "The Sermon on the Mount" was not like any sermon she had ever heard. Admittedly her experience in such matters was limited but she could see that there were at least seven separate units and she also discovered, on her own, that bits of the "Sermon" were scattered through the other Gospels in a disconnected fashion. It gave her some solace to discover later that she was making the right judgement: that "The Sermon on the Mount" was in fact a collection of the sayings of Jesus that must have been given at different times and to different audiences. This would explain why Jesus could be talking about the permanence of the Law (of Moses) at one time and, at another, giving instructions which seemed to allow for contradiction to the Law, such as the prohibition of oath taking.

She also had a feeling that the Sermon on the Mount was awkwardly placed: at the end of Chapter 4 of Matthew is the summary of the healing ministry, then three chapters devoted to the Sermon, and finally in Chapter 8, three specific examples of healings. It was as though Matthew had this collection of sayings and was uncertain where to put it.

But when Tuesday came along again, as it did on a regular basis, she felt more comfortable with herself and had decided how she would handle the next session. Webster had been in touch and asked for a little time for his precious Parallels, this time to give Luke's version of the Beatitudes. He had gone to the trouble of preparing the text to be included in her PowerPoint presentation. Melanie was somewhat concerned, feeling that Matthew's Gospel was more than enough without distracting their thoughts by comparisons. But, out of her regard for Webster, she had agreed and determined that she would make it clear that this wasn't to be a regular occurrence. Really, Webster could be a bit of a nuisance!

After the preliminaries, she urged them to put to one side conventional thinking about the "Sermon"; for example, the idea that Jesus was somehow following Moses "up the mountain" and coming down with a new Law. "It's really not a sermon at all. It's a kind of anthology of the sayings of Jesus, delivered at different times and to different situations. Maybe the writer of Matthew's Gospel contrived a context for the whole collection rather than have them unattached to any historical setting." There was some muted grumbling that she was rather imposing her ideas ahead of time. "All right," she conceded, "let's take a look."

And there on the screen they could consider the first section:

> *Seeing the multitude of people, Jesus went up the hill. There he seated himself, and when his disciples came to him, he proceeded to teach them, and said:*
>
> *"Blessed are the poor in spirit, for to them belongs the Kingdom of Heaven.*
>
> *Blessed are the mourners, for they shall be comforted.*
>
> *Blessed are the meek, for they shall obtain possession of the earth.*
>
> *Blessed are those who hunger and thirst for righteousness, for they shall be completely satisfied.*
>
> *Blessed are the compassionate, for they shall receive compassion.*
>
> *Blessed are the pure in heart, for they shall see God.*

> *Blessed are the peacemakers, for it is they who will be recognized as sons of God.*
>
> *Blessed are those who have borne persecution in the cause of righteousness, for to them belongs the Kingdom of Heaven.*
>
> *Blessed are you when they have insulted and persecuted you, and have said every cruel thing about you falsely for my sake.*
>
> *Be joyful and triumphant, because your reward is great in heaven; for so were the Prophets before you persecuted."*

Nine parallel statements of blessing ("The Beatitudes"); there was general agreement that the last two suggested a context of violent opposition, more appropriate to later times, even into the experience of the early church.

Webster was anxious to have his say. He pointed out that the hypothesis that the "Sermon" was an anthology could be argued from the occurrence of several of its verses appearing in other Gospels, in a completely different context. "There are many examples," he said. "Here's one: the teaching in Chapter 7 about prayer appears, word for word, in Luke's Gospel after the parable of the Friend at Midnight (Luke 11)." Much to Melanie's relief, he continued with the concession: "It would be too much to go through all such examples but rather than take my word for it, check them out." Several in the group, including Al, had followed his urging and now possessed copies of the Parallels, checked out Matthew 7 as he spoke and agreed with his findings.

But he was eager to show something else: the parallel section of Luke's Gospel which now, thanks to PowerPoint, appeared on the screen:

> *Then fixing his eyes upon his disciples, Jesus said to them,*
> *"Blessed are you poor, because the Kingdom of God is yours.*
>
> *Blessed are you who hunger now, because your hunger shall be satisfied. Blessed are you who now weep aloud, because you shall laugh.*
>
> *Blessed are you when men shall hate you and exclude you from their society and insult you, and spurn your very names as evil things, for the Son of Man's sake.*
>
> *Be glad at such a time, and dance for joy; for your reward is great in Heaven; for that is just the way their forefathers behaved to the Prophets!"*

"I am convinced that Luke's version is closer to the original. Matthew tried to widen the application of the teaching." He pointed out that "blessed are you poor" made sense as addressed to those who came out to hear him, while "blessed are the poor" seemed much more difficult, suggesting that poverty was somehow beneficial. It would be natural to try to escape this difficulty by making the change from "the poor" to "the poor in spirit."

But by now, Al was barely concealing his impatience. "What you have said is interesting but is way ahead of where I am. I need to know what the very first verse means; what does 'blessed' mean and who are the 'poor' and then this 'Kingdom of God,' we haven't got far in understanding that!"

Help was on its way! Several expressed opinions about the meaning of "blessed" and a consensus emerged that it was along the lines of being favored, or even honored, by God. Andrew, who was keen on the translation called the New English Bible, chimed in that the paraphrase, "Blessed are those who know they have a need for God" was the reading given there.

As for the "poor," Martha claimed that it meant those completely without resources, those dependant on the charity of others. "It's hard for us to envision third world poverty," she said. "Try to imagine living on one or two dollars a day. Franz Fanon wrote a book, 'The Wretched of the Earth' and its title has stuck in my mind. Maybe, such people are praised because they are more likely to become dependant on the generosity of God," she suggested.

As for the "Kingdom of God," Melanie reminded them of some of the options she had laid out during the previous week's discussion and urged them to be patient. "Perhaps," she said, "the purpose of the Gospel is to lead the reader gradually into an understanding of the concept, even to know what it means to participate in something only gradually understood." She urged them to look at the other verses and see how exactly alien to modern culture they were. Blessedness of the sorrowful and the meek falls uncomfortably on modern ears. She recalled Mark Twain's dismissal of the Beatitudes as "immense sarcasms."

She realized yet again how difficult it was to do any kind of justice to the whole chapter in the two hours available and regretfully clicked onto the next section:

> "You are the salt of the earth; but if salt has become tasteless, in what way can it regain its saltiness? It is no longer good for anything but to be thrown away and trodden on by the passers by.
>
> You are the light of the world; a town cannot be hid if built on a hilltop.
>
> Nor is a lamp lighted to be put under a bushel, but on the lampstand; and then it gives light to all in the house.
>
> Just so let your light shine before all men, in order that they may see your holy lives and may give glory to your Father who is in Heaven."

It was a relief to encounter something a bit more straightforward. She could get away with a reminder of the value of salt in the ancient world. Andrew made the helpful comment: "I am surprised that the statements are so definite. 'You are the salt' and 'You are the light' could be seen as a bit of wishful thinking." He paused. "Or perhaps Jesus saw potential in unlikely people." Stephen suggested that it might have been addressed to the disciples. "You can't get more 'unlikely' than that". Al apologized that they had passed over the section in Chapter 4 about the calling of the disciples. "Evidently they were an unpromising bunch," he said.

Pushing ahead, Melanie displayed the next section:

> "Do not for a moment suppose that I have come to abrogate the Law or the Prophets: I have not come to abrogate them but to give them their completion.
>
> Solemnly I tell you that until Heaven and earth pass away, not one iota or smallest detail will pass away from the Law until all has taken place.
>
> Whoever therefore breaks one of these least commandments and teaches others to break them, will be called the least in the Kingdom of Heaven; but whoever practices them and teaches them, he will be acknowledged as great in the Kingdom of Heaven.
>
> For I assure you that unless your righteousness greatly surpasses that of the Scribes and the Pharisees, you will certainly not find entrance into the Kingdom of Heaven."

It was easy to understand the idea of Jesus giving the Law its completion but there was much debate about the apparent insistence on keeping the Law in every detail. Stephen knew that there were six hundred and thirteen commandments of the Law. Melanie was afraid that he might want to recite them all. But he contented himself with the question: "Does this mean that modern day followers of Jesus should follow them all, including keeping the seventh day rather than the first? Should we all become Seventh Day Adventists? And what about the Kosher food regulations?" Martha wondered if this was part of the Sermon on the Mount comes from a very early period when Jesus thought of himself as nothing more than a reformer of Judaism. "Later in the Gospel," she said, "Jesus brings a child forward as a model of the Kingdom. You know the bit where he says 'unless you repent and become as this little child, you will never enter the Kingdom.' The child is the least likely person to be meticulous in the keeping of the Law and its commandments."

Again it was necessary to move along, with a reminder from Melanie that their discussions were meant to open doors on various possibilities and that reading during the week would make a big difference. "I sound like my Grade 9 English teacher," she lamented.

So now it was time to look at the section which dealt with "anger management":

> "You have heard that it was said to the ancients, 'Thou shalt not commit murder' and whoever commits murder will be answerable to the magistrate.
>
> But I say to you that every one who becomes angry with his brother shall be answerable to the magistrate; that whoever says to his brother 'Raca,' shall be answerable to the Sanhedrin; and that whoever says, 'You fool!' shall be liable to the Gehenna of fire.
>
> If therefore when you are offering your gift upon the altar, you remember that your brother has a grievance against you, leave your gift there before the altar, and go and make friends with your brother first, and then return and proceed to offer your gift.
>
> Come to terms without delay with your opponent while you are yet with him on the way to the court; for fear he should obtain judgement from the magistrate against you, and the magistrate should give you in custody to the officer and you be thrown into prison. I solemnly tell you that you will certainly not be released till you have paid the very last penny."

There was much discussion. Did the text imply that the thought or the word of violence was as bad as the act itself? Surely, there was no way to avoid the thought and resisting it was the essence of virtue? As Andrew said, "It sets the bar too high!"

Someone had discovered that "Raca" meant something like "blockhead" and commented that it was an Aramaic word. This gave rise to discussion about the language which Jesus spoke and the reference to scholarly opinion that it was Aramaic at home and probably Greek in the marketplace. Webster (again!): "Did you know that 'Gehenna' refers to the Valley of Hinnon where the city of Jerusalem disposed of its rubbish. Evidently, it was a scary place where fires burned constantly. Among other things, bodies of dead criminals ended up in the valley of Hinnon. Jerusalem must have been a smelly, smoky city!"

Melanie was interested in the role of the law courts, as though the teachings of Jesus might be enforceable by law. They agreed that it was all a bit mysterious.

Al asked about gifts at the altar. "Should the church reject a gift from someone if they know that there is an unresolved conflict? I wonder if any church practices such a policy?" They all agreed that it was unlikely!

Some similar comments were made about the next section:

"You have heard that it was said, 'Thou shalt not commit adultery.'

But I tell you that whoever looks at a woman and cherishes lustful thoughts has already in his heart become guilty with regard to her. If therefore your eye, even the right eye, is a snare to you, tear it out and away with it; it is better for you that one member should be destroyed rather than that your whole body should be thrown into Gehenna. And if your right hand is a snare to you, cut it off and away with it; it is better for you that one member should be destroyed rather than that your whole body should go into Gehenna.

It was also said, 'If any man puts away his wife, let him give her a written notice of divorce.' But I tell you that every man who puts away his wife except on the ground of unfaithfulness causes her to commit adultery, and whoever marries her when so divorced commits adultery."

It was clear that the prohibition of the "lustful thought" went far beyond anything in the Law of Moses and the proposed remedies were judged to be extreme. Melanie remarked that she had heard the occasional comment, "I don't go to church but I try to live by the Sermon on the Mount" and she now wondered if the speaker of such an opinion had even read the text. Stephen, who had grown up Lutheran, recalled, "In our Catechism class, we were taught Luther's view that the Sermon was designed to propose an impossible demand which would lead us to throw ourselves on God's mercy." Some commented that "impossible" might be the right word but it might lead to despair or even to indifference.

Martha reminded the group of the long history of struggle within the church on the question of divorce and that the phrase "except on the ground of unfaithfulness" doesn't appear in the parallel passages in Mark and Luke. She spoke sharply. "The possibility of a woman needing to find relief in divorce seems not to be addressed, either by Moses or by Jesus. I wonder how much of this text we are looking at is church teaching from the first century and how much truly goes back to Jesus. He was in very many ways sympathetic to the situation of women. It sounds more like the church!" She also wanted the group to be aware of the long section in Matthew 19 about divorce and wondered if it would be helpful to include it in the present discussion. Melanie had not considered this but realized how complicated the discussions would become if later parts were included. "Maybe when we come to Matthew 19, we can refer to this part of the Sermon on the Mount. Martha, could you remind us when we get there." But Martha wasn't quite finished. "Do you remember that I suggested that 'Matthew' might be a woman? You might think that this passage supports that idea. But I'm not sure that it does. Mark and Luke include it so it seems to be part of the common tradition." Stephen couldn't resist. "Maybe they were all women," he suggested. Al admitted that the whole thing left him confused. "How does the man's action, 'putting away his wife', cause her to commit adultery?" No one could think of an answer so Melanie moved them along to the next section:

> *"Again, you have heard that it was said to the ancients, 'Thou shalt not swear falsely, but shalt perform thy vows to the Lord.' But I tell you not to swear at all; neither by Heaven, for it is God's throne; nor by the earth, for it is the footstool under his feet; nor by Jerusalem, for it is the City of the Great King. And do not swear by your head, for you cannot make one hair white or black. But let*

your language be, 'Yes, yes,' or 'No, no.' Anything in excess of this comes from the Evil One."

"Here's my problem," she said. "In Deuteronomy 6.13, the law is: *Thou shalt fear the Lord thy God, and serve Him, and shalt swear by His Name.* Having forbidden his hearers to change one jot or tittle of the law, Jesus does exactly that. I like Martha's suggestion about different stages."

Some one said. "Martha, tell us again." So she repeated her idea that the early Jesus might have seen himself as a reformer of Judaism and only later, felt free to make changes, even to the Law.

Again with an eye on the clock, Melanie moved relentlessly onward:

"You have heard that it was said, 'Eye for eye, tooth for tooth.'

But I tell you not to resist a wicked man, but if any one strikes you on the right cheek, turn the other to him as well.

If any one wishes to go to law with you and to deprive you of your under garment, let him take your outer one also.

And whoever shall compel you to convey his goods one mile, go with him two.

To him who asks, give: from him who would borrow, turn not away.

You have heard that it was said, 'Thou shalt love thy neighbour and hate thine enemy.' But I command you all, love your enemies, and pray for your persecutors; that so you may become true sons of your Father in Heaven; for he causes his sun to rise on the wicked as well as the good, and sends rain upon those who do right and those who do wrong. For if you love only those who love you, what reward have you earned? Do not even the tax-gatherers do that? And if you salute only your near relatives, what praise is due to you? Do not even the Gentiles do the same?

You, however, are to be complete in goodness, as your Heavenly Father is complete."

Again it was recognized that the requirements of the Law were being altered and a code of behavior proposed which most Christians over the centuries had chosen to ignore. Al reminded them of the Christian communities who had practiced pacifism. "At one time I was active in the Peace Movements in Australia, especially Anzac Ploughshares. They were very keen on this passage." The whole question of non-violent protest, Tolstoy, Gandhi and Martin Luther King, and "just war theology" became the focus for a vigorous debate which engaged almost everyone and led to a tongue-in-cheek comment from Webster. "Melanie, it would be the perfect topic when you make your choice for next year." Eventually, Melanie was able to lead them back to the text and the question of whether the teaching of Jesus about violence was intended to provide more than a personal guide for his disciples.

The evening ended with Stephen explaining, "I have heard an argument that Jesus was proposing an 'interim ethic' for the short time remaining before the Kingdom of God would be made visible." But it was too late since the debate on pacifism had filled everyone's minds and questions of the sort that he was advancing would have to wait until another day.

As she left, she thought of Martha's reference to Chapter 19. It seemed infinitely remote and she wondered if she would have the stamina for this whole lengthy business. She dredged up a memory of the saying that no one, putting hands to the plough and looking back, is fit for the Kingdom of Heaven. "It's not the looking back that's my problem," she murmured.

Chapter 6

Thursday 9.30 am. Dull skies and a lengthy meeting with the Bishop and the Chancellor. About a severance package for an errant priest who would take early retirement, but at a price. At least, thought Melanie, not errors of the sexual variety, but distasteful nonetheless.

As they separated, the Bishop asked for a "private word" and they sat down in Melanie's cramped office. "I need your opinion about Alexander Vernon," began the Bishop. She was for a moment startled to hear Al being described thus and wondered what information she could or should provide. "You know, of course, that he's in Matty's group and so I see him once a week." The Bishop grinned at her; "It's Melanie's group now! I hear nothing but good about it." She wondered how much he knew but decided to tell most of what she knew about Al: "He's been a good influence on us because it's all new to him. He asks the basic questions we feel embarrassed to raise. He is smart and does his homework. And he was in last year's men's group."

The Bishop hesitated and then said, "You probably don't know that Al's father is an Archdeacon in Adelaide. He's written to me to see if Al is settling down here." Melanie expressed surprise at this, recalling Al's statement that he had not been baptized. "Yes," the Bishop replied, "that surprises me too but Al's parents separated before he was born and he was raised by his mother who was quite hostile to the Church." He also explained that Al's uncle had owned the bookstore and the building which housed it and that Al had inherited the whole thing, every brick and every book. "Lucky man," she replied. "All I inherited from Aunt Matty was her group!"

That evening, with thoughts of Aunt Matty, she ventured into the package again, thinking as she did so, that she should be courageous and go through the whole collection. But for now she was content to come across a small booklet, "The Prayers of Jesus" by a German scholar, Joachim Jeremias. She was relieved to discover that it was readable and that it gave her some good ideas for the upcoming session which would include the Lord's Prayer as part of the text.

So on the following Tuesday, she looked around the group with some confidence that she was well prepared. Here was the first section, up and ready:

> *"But beware of doing your good actions in the sight of men, in order to attract their gaze; if you do, there is no reward for you with your Father who is in Heaven. When you give in charity, never blow a trumpet before you as the hypocrites do in the synagogues and streets in order that their praises may be sung by men. I solemnly tell you that they already have their reward. But when you are giving in charity, let not your left hand perceive what your right hand is doing, that your charities may be in secret; and then your Father—he who sees in secret—will recompense you."*

No one had much trouble with this. But Stephen remarked his surprise, "That bit about the left hand not knowing what the right hand is doing. I had always used it as a negative!" Now, however, all were eager to get on, with considerable anticipation, for the next section:

> *"And when praying, you must not be like the hypocrites. They are fond of standing and praying in the synagogues or at the corners of the wider streets, in order that men may see them. I solemnly tell you that they already have their reward. But you, whenever you pray, go into your own room and shut the door: then pray to your Father who is in secret, and your Father—he who sees in secret—will recompense you. And when praying, do not use needless repetitions as the Gentiles do, for they expect to be listened to because of their multitude of words. Do not, however, imitate them; for your Father knows what things you need before ever you ask him.*
>
> *In this manner therefore pray:*
>
> *Our Father who art in Heaven, may Thy name be kept holy; let Thy kingdom come; let Thy will be done, as in Heaven so on earth; give us to-day our bread for the day; and forgive us our shortcomings, as we also have forgiven those who have failed in their duty towards us; and bring us not into temptation, but rescue us from the Evil one.*

For if you forgive others their offences, your Heavenly Father will forgive you also; but if you do not forgive others their offences, neither will your Father forgive yours."

Before the discussion of the Lord's Prayer, Al asked," What can he mean when he says that your Father knows what things you need before ever you ask. That seems to undercut the whole business of prayer." There were various opinions but in the end it was agreed that Jesus practiced a life of prayer and insisted upon it for his followers. There was some sense that prayer was a problem for all present and that they could spend a whole year on it. "Maybe," said Stephen, "the year after next . . . !" and Melanie had this vision of an endless succession of topics unfolding, one after another; and she didn't have a niece to whom she could pass along the family business!

They were all more or less aware of the variety of interpretations of the Lord's Prayer. Webster had his oar in the water before any of the others, to tell them of Luke's version. "In that case, the Prayer is given in a shorter form in answer to the request from the disciples: 'John taught his disciples to pray; Lord, teach us to pray'" He urged upon them the idea that Luke's version was likely closer to the original but there was some contrary opinion that Jesus might have, in fact, given the Prayer in two forms in two different circumstances. Webster was not easily put off. "Look," he said, " the version in Luke's Gospel is so short: *Father, hallowed be your name; your Kingdom come. Give us each day our daily bread. Forgive us our sins, for we also forgive everyone who sins against us. And lead us not into temptation.*" Melanie took some pleasure in his surprise when she put up exactly those words on the screen. By now she could anticipate his line of thought. But his argument that "shorter means earlier" left some scratching their heads.

There was a question that the familiar doxology, "For thine is the Kingdom, the power and the glory for ever and ever. Amen" was not included; the answer seemed to be that the earliest manuscripts didn't include it and that it was understandable that something was added later to rescue the prayer from its abrupt ending.

Melanie reminded them of the usual interpretation of the Lord's Prayer as a "family prayer," using the first word "Father" to point in that direction. She also said, "I have from Aunt Matty a little book by the German scholar, Jeremias. It's about the Lord's Prayer and I was amazed that he spent fifty five pages to explore the use of the word, 'Abba.'" They were mostly familiar with the Aramaic original "Abba": a most intimate form of address used in the family by even the youngest child. "I can't summarize the discussion but Jeremias convinced me that 'Abba' was a unique form of address, unknown and even somewhat scandalous in the Judaism of those times." Al wondered if Jesus, perhaps growing up without a father, might have been compensating for that loss. Melanie thought of her knowledge of Al's early life, knowledge that made his suggestion rather powerful. But Webster was quick to respond, "It's an interesting idea, Al. Certainly Joseph disappears from the text very early. But he was evidently still around when they made the trip to Jerusalem when Jesus was twelve years old. That is, if Luke got that right."

Melanie pushed ahead: " Getting back to 'Abba', it is easy to interpret the remainder of the Prayer in the light of that single word: a longing for the reign of God, a petition for the daily necessities of life and a prayer for forgiveness and a path free from temptation. The only surprising aspect is the way in which forgiveness is linked to the willingness to forgive others; Matthew's text even goes so far as to underline this: 'If you do not forgive . . . neither will you be forgiven . . . '"

She paused, realizing that she was lecturing. "The trouble is," she confessed, "I've been reading again!" Martha encouraged her to continue; "You'd better get it off your chest!"

So she continued, assuring them that she would only take a couple more minutes. "There is a whole other way of looking at the Prayer which sees the Lord's Prayer as related to the coming of the Kingdom by Divine intervention into human history. Even the familiar 'daily bread' can be given another meaning; the word translated 'daily' is much debated and there is convincing evidence that the translation, 'Give us today the bread of Tomorrow' is to be preferred, where the 'Tomorrow' is the great tomorrow of the Kingdom. So that part of the prayer is seen as a plea that in daily life they might participate in the Divine Banquet which is a part of the expectation. And, anticipating forgiveness in the Age to Come, there is the present forgiving and offering forgiveness to others. Finally, as some of the modern translations already have given us, the final petition is 'Bring us not to the time of trial but deliver us from the Evil One,' praying that they might escape the final persecution of God's people."

There was a pause until it was clear that she had finished. Then Al said, "My business would fail if people didn't read so you won't get any complaint from me. But the second interpretation is strange to modern ears. Did Jesus really believe that he was announcing the end of the world, like some weird character on a street corner?" This question hung over the group for a while and no one had an answer. There was the sense that this question would come up again and again.

"So," thought Melanie, "when in doubt, push on!" and so she did, with the next section of this long chapter now on display:

> "When any of you fast, never assume gloomy looks as the hypocrites do; for they disfigure their faces in order that it may be evident to men that they are fasting. I solemnly tell you that they already have their reward. But, whenever you fast, pour perfume on your hair and wash your face, that it may not be apparent to men that you are fasting, but to your Father who is in secret; and your Father—he who sees in secret—will recompense you
>
> Do not lay up stores of wealth for yourselves on earth, where the moth and wear-and-tear destroy, and where thieves break in and steal. But amass wealth for yourselves in Heaven, where neither the moth nor wear-and-tear destroys, and where thieves do not break in and steal. For where your wealth is, there also will your heart be."

There was an almost audible sigh of relief; they could cope with this and the discussion took a predictable path; some talk about fasting with reminiscences of Lents gone by. And some reflections on the concept of voluntary poverty, or at least restraint, in the accumulation of possessions.

Just as they were feeling on easy terms with the text, she threw up the next bit:

> *The eye is the lamp of the body. If then your eye is good, your whole body will be well lighted; but if your eye is bad, your whole body will be dark. If however the very light within you is darkness, how dense must the darkness be!*

There were looks of puzzlement which she helped out by commenting that she had read that the "good eye" was synonymous with generosity and that therefore the text followed on from the previous section- an exhortation to generosity. Someone wondered if the "light within" might mean generosity towards oneself; if this is lacking then the verdict, "how dense must the darkness be" seemed to make sense. But there was some skepticism about this interpretation. Those who were looking at the next verse in their Bibles saw that it was a continuation of the argument about the use of wealth and possessions and used this to argue that the "good eye" section must refer to generosity to the poor.

Melanie put up this familiar text:

> "No man can be the bondservant of two masters; for either he will dislike one and like the other, or he will attach himself to one and think slightingly of the other. You cannot be the bondservants both of God and of possessions."

Then she was eager to move on to the section on anxiety, remarking that for an era sometimes called "The Age of Anxiety," this was a timely piece:

> "For this reason I charge you not to be over-anxious about your lives, inquiring what you are to eat or what you are to drink, nor yet about your bodies, inquiring what clothes you are to put on. Is not the life more precious than its food, and the body than its clothing? Look at the birds which fly in the air: they do not sow or reap or store up in barns, but your Heavenly Father feeds them: are not you of much greater value than they?
>
> Which of you by being over-anxious can add a single foot to his height? And why be anxious about clothing? Learn a lesson from the wild lilies. Watch their growth. They neither toil nor spin, and yet I tell you that not even Solomon in all his magnificence could array himself like one of these. And if God so clothes the wild herbage which to-day flourishes and to-morrow is thrown into the oven, is it not much more certain that He will clothe you, you men of little faith?
>
> Do not be over-anxious, therefore, asking "What shall we eat?" or "What shall we drink?" or "What shall we wear?" For all these are questions that Gentiles are always asking; but your Heavenly Father knows that you need these things—all of them.
>
> But make his Kingdom and righteousness your chief aim, and then these things shall all be given you in addition. Do not be

over-anxious, therefore, about to-morrow, for to-morrow will bring its own cares. Enough for each day are its own troubles."

She thought that there wouldn't be much discussion on this since it was straightforward and might send them off with something to ponder. Stephen, however, wished to report on a sermon he had heard the previous Sunday on the phrase, "You of little faith." They listened with some impatience but then with growing interest as he explained that in the original Greek the phrase was one word "oligopistoi"; "I am rather proud to be able to remember it since otherwise I know no Greek. It might be something like "little faithers" if such a construction were possible in English. Jesus applied this word several times to the disciples, maybe teasingly. It dawned on me that maybe Jesus was sometimes teasing his friends!" He paused to let that sink in. "In contrast, those commended for great faith were two Gentiles, one the Roman centurion and the other the Syro-Phoenician woman. We'll meet them later. Anyhow, the point of the sermon was the saying that faith as little as a grain of mustard seed would suffice for mighty works." Webster interrupted, "We'll meet that later, too." "So," concluded Stephen, "we went away from church, encouraged that there was still hope for us."

And with those words in mind, they went their separate ways.

Chapter 7

IT IS NOT so widely known that there are monastic communities in the Anglican tradition. Melanie knew that the Community of St. Saviour had been important in her aunt's life. (The good ladies insisted on the English spelling of "Saviour". They enjoyed their little joke: "our Saviour includes you!"). For a number of years, Melanie had acted as their legal advisor.

On that next Friday, she conferred with Mother Agnes over some property matters and, when finished, she asked for some time on a more personal level. She explained how Matty's will had left her an unwanted "bequest." She paused and then confessed, "I'm really struggling to keep going. Maybe I should just give it up." She was surprised at her own words; she hadn't quite realized until that moment her own discomfort. Agnes kept silence for several moments and asked if some single issue had brought her to this realization. "I suppose Matthew and the parts about prayer, to tell the truth. I don't pray and never have . . . am I missing something? And it's so confusing," she continued, "this talk firstly that the Father knows what we need but that we should ask anyhow; and the unblushing promises that, whatever we ask for, we will get. It's all so strange to me." Agnes smiled and replied, "Maybe you raise this with me because prayer is what I do. Let me tell you, I am just as puzzled as when I was a novice. But we keep going. Do you know the Rapunzel poem? R.S.Thomas took an old story and gave it a new twist." Melanie remembered the fairy story: the princess imprisoned in the tower and the prince who climbs to her rescue, using her long braided hair as a ladder. "But I don't see how . . . it seems hard to make a connection with prayer." Mother Agnes smiled. "It takes a poet to do that! He imagines prayers are like gravel, flung at the window to attract attention. But no response, no plaited ladder, only silence. He ends the little poem by admitting that he would long ago have given up, "except that once he thought he saw the movement of the curtain."

Melanie went away, none the wiser but considerably sadder. Had Mother Agnes told her this as a reflection on her own experience? Or just to remind Melanie of her own situation?

That evening, as she sat down at her solitary table, she remembered those many meals with Matty and the grace that Matty insisted upon before eating. She said it again for the first time since she had been alone, feeling rather foolish. Then for the first time, she wept for her own loneliness and for the absence of Matty.

Throughout the next few days, she thought of Rapunzel, imprisoned in her tower but her mind kept repeating the phrase which Mother Agnes had used, "But we keep going," and slowly thoughts of quitting faded away. So, by Tuesday, she felt revived and ready to face more of the Sermon. She reminded the group that this was the last section and admitted that her own experience of the Sermon had been one of exasperation; "So often, it seems out of touch with everyday experience and maybe that's the point. Perhaps it's meant to startle us out of the commonplace." It was time to get started:

> "Judge not, that you may not be judged; for your own judgement will be dealt—and your own measure assigned—to yourselves. And why do you look at the splinter in your brother's eye, and not notice the beam which is in your own eye? Or how say to your brother, "Allow me to take the splinter out of your eye," while the beam is in your own eye? Hypocrite, first take the beam out of your own eye, and then you will see clearly how to remove the splinter from your brother's eye."

Stephen protested that Jesus seemed to be proposing a standard that he himself did not keep. The whole Sermon is filled with judgements about human conduct, that anger was equivalent to murder, that the lustful thought was equivalent to adultery and so on. And throughout the Gospel, judgements directed against scribes, Pharisees and others. There were some floundering attempts to explain this anomaly. Webster came closest when he said, "Maybe we are too quick to assume that all these sayings have universal application. We don't know the situation in which this one was said; perhaps to a group of disciples who were experiencing dissension and finger-pointing. In such a context, it would make sense."

And with that interesting possibility, they were content to plod on:

> "Give not that which is holy to the dogs, nor throw your pearls to the swine; otherwise they will trample them under their feet and then turn and attack you."

There was some awareness that "dogs" was a word often applied to Gentiles. Martha was eager to point ahead to Matthew 15 with its account of Jesus meeting a Gentile woman, whose request was rebuffed by the reply, "It is not right to take the children's food and toss it to the dogs." So it was agreed that the saying probably was given in a similar context.

But it wasn't going to be easy to fit the next section into any context:

> "Ask, and it will be given to you; seek, and you will find; knock, and the door will be opened to you. For it is always he who asks that receives, he who seeks that finds, and he who knocks that has the door opened to him. What man is there among you, who if his son shall ask him for bread will offer him a stone? Or if the son shall ask him for a fish will offer him a snake? If you then, imperfect as you are, know how to give good gifts to your children, how much more will your Father in Heaven give good things to those who ask him!"

Melanie conceded her personal bewilderment about this, a seemingly unqualified promise that all the disciple needed to do was to ask. No faith needed, just a willingness to ask, to seek, to knock. "It didn't help," she said, "when I consulted someone who had devoted her whole life to prayer, someone who confessed to being still totally in the dark about this passage." She looked around, hoping for new insights. Someone suggested that the succession, "Ask . . . seek . . . knock . . ." might suggest the need for persistence and this was followed up by the reference to Luke's Gospel where Jesus is recorded as having given a parable "to show them that they should always pray and not give up." But generally this was thought to be at odds with the idea of the child asking the parent for bread or fish; surely no need for persistent pleading! Finally, Andrew came up with a more likely explanation: "When children ask, they don't always get what they ask for. So perhaps 'Ask and it shall be given to you' can be seen as a promise that there will always be a response but not necessarily exactly what was requested. Maybe a case of 'Father knows best' " There was more sympathy to this idea although, as Martha pointed out, it wouldn't be much comfort to a mother praying daily for the safe return of her husband away at the wars, and then to receive the dreaded telegram. Could it ever be possible to comfort such a one with the notion that God has something better in store? Andrew conceded that his idea wouldn't fly in that situation and the conversation lapsed into incoherence.

They were glad to move on:

> "Everything, therefore, be it what it may, that you would have men do to you, do you also the same to them; for in this the Law and the Prophets are summed up."

The Golden Rule was familiar and seemed to return them to solid ground. Stephen remembered that George Bernard Shaw had criticized the Golden Rule on the grounds that "people have different tastes." Someone was rash enough to ask for details of this idea! Stephen was willing to oblige. "Suppose you shared an office with a colleague and you had a taste for classical music. So you kept your radio tuned to a classical music station. In so doing, you gave your colleague a steady dose of Mozart; you would be giving as you would hope to receive. But your colleague's taste in music was for jazz and he hated your choice. This is essentially Shaw's criticism." He paused, but only for breath. "Of course, you only need to apply the Rule in a different way and it works well: your music causes offence, you wouldn't wish to be offended so you turn the radio off." Melanie quickly led the discussion forward, remarking that the remainder of the Sermon was a kind of summary

> "Enter by the narrow gate; for wide is the gate and broad the road which leads to ruin, and many there are who enter by it; because small is the gate and narrow the road which leads to life, and few are those who find it.
>
> Beware of the false teachers—men who come to you in sheep's fleeces, but beneath that disguise they are ravenous wolves. By their fruits you will easily recognize them. Are grapes gathered from thorns or figs from brambles? Just so every good tree produces "good fruit", but a poisonous tree produces bad fruit. A good tree cannot bear bad fruit, nor a poisonous tree good fruit. Every tree which does not yield good fruit is cut down and thrown aside for burning. So by their fruits at any rate, you will easily recognize them.

> *Not every one who says to me, 'Master, Master,' will enter the Kingdom of Heaven, but only those who are obedient to my Father who is in Heaven. Many will say to me on that day, 'Master, Master, have we not prophesied in Thy name, and in Thy name expelled demons, and in Thy name performed many mighty works?' And then I will tell them plainly, 'I never knew you: begone from me, you doers of wickedness.'*
>
> *Every one who hears these my teachings and acts upon them will be found to resemble a wise man who builds his house upon rock; and the heavy rain falls, the swollen torrents come, and the winds blow and beat against the house; yet it does not fall, for its foundation is on rock. And every one who hears these my teachings and does not act upon them will be found to resemble a fool who builds his house upon sand. The heavy rain descends, the swollen torrents come, and the winds blow and burst upon the house, and it falls; and disastrous is the fall."*

For time's sake, they looked at it all at one viewing and saw how the Judgement section "Not everyone who says to me . . . ." could be seen as surprising. It certainly suggested a later part of the ministry of Jesus where he identifies himself as presiding over the Day of Judgement. In fact a large part of scholarly opinion would regard this section as an interpolation from the teaching of the early church. It also seemed contrary to the previous teaching about the good and evil trees; surely "prophesying in your Name" and "casting out demons" would qualify as "good fruit." Thus the evening ended, as was so often the case, with much to puzzle over and they left with the final piece of editorial summary still in their minds:

> *When Jesus had concluded this discourse, the crowds were filled with amazement at his teaching, for he had been teaching them as one who had authority, and not as their Scribes taught.*

Chapter 8

SHE'D BEEN PUTTING IT off for a while but that weekend Melanie knew it was time to visit her father. He had been in a care home now for three years, suffering from a mysterious form of dementia. Sometimes he was perfectly rational and they could converse as though nothing was wrong; at other times, he didn't know her, or, worse still, thought that she was his long-dead wife.

He had decided, years before, when some premonition of his future came to him, that he wanted to be in a church-run home, several hour's drive away. The distance gave her some excuse for not visiting more often, but she knew how she dreaded the visits. This time, as she entered his room, clutching flowers in a sweaty hand, it was a great relief that he greeted her with every appearance of normality. She greeted him warmly and they were soon engaged in conversation that inevitably led into a discussion of her "legacy." It was the first time she had been able to tell him the story and he laughed, rather more than was necessary, she thought. She wondered whether he had been a party to the scheme. She described the group and their struggles with Matthew, hoping that he might enjoy some conversation on some of the issues. "Next Tuesday," she said, "we begin Chapter 8 with all the healing miracles. It will be difficult for me to hide my skepticism. Do you think that such things really happened?" He was silent for a while and she thought that his mind might be wandering off, away from her. But he replied, "What kind of evidence would convince you? There are many unexplained recoveries on record, 'spontaneous remissions' in the medical parlance. But it can be argued that this merely indicates that science hasn't fully understood natural processes. I can remember quite a few situations when people prayed, someone recovered and there was rejoicing that prayer had been answered. But many more when people prayed . . ." His voice trailed off and she knew he was thinking about her mother.

"But," she said, "these healings don't always seem to be the result of prayer. Is it possible that some people have special powers?" There was a long silence and she knew that his moment of lucidity was fading. Their visit became one of idle chatter on her part and increasingly irrelevant responses on his, until she was glad to leave. Her own question, " Is it possible that some people have special powers?" echoed in her mind as she drove home.

When they gathered on Tuesday evening, Melanie began by congratulating them on successfully navigating the shoals and rapids of the Sermon. "We left a lot undecided," she said, "but we gave it our best shot." Then she reminded them that, immediately before the Sermon, there was the summary of the ministry of Jesus: ". . . they brought all the sick to him . . . and he cured them." She was then able to introduce Chapter 8 with its specific examples. Firstly:

> *Upon descending from the hill country, he was followed by immense crowds. And a leper came to him, and throwing himself at his feet, said, "Sir, if only you are willing, you are able to cleanse me." So Jesus put out his hand and touched him, and said, "I am willing: be cleansed." Instantly he was cleansed from his leprosy; and Jesus said to him, "Be careful to tell no one, but go and show yourself to the priest, and offer the gift, which Moses appointed as evidence for them."*

They had all done their homework and wanted to discuss their feelings about the existence of "special powers." Some felt that since Jesus was "special," even "divine," it would make sense that he could do such things. There was reference to the long tradition of spiritual healers, shamans and others, throughout all cultures. Then, inevitably, to TV evangelists and their claims. Al mentioned James Randi, a famous debunker of such claims but it was agreed that even if spiritual healing attracted all sorts of dishonesty, the tradition couldn't be easily dismissed.

As for the text on display, Webster drew their attention to the instruction, "Be careful to tell no-one" and gave them a brief introduction to the idea of the "Messianic Secret": that, from time to time, Jesus instructs the beneficiaries of healing miracles to keep silent. "But," he said, "an instruction like that fits awkwardly into the text; on the one hand, 'immense crowds' who presumably viewed the miracle, and on the other, the attempt to keep the matter secret."

They heard him out patiently but it was clear that the question that had remained in Melanie's mind since her visit to her father was one which they shared in common: Is it possible that some people have special powers? The discussion was, as usual, inconclusive. The question would come up again and again.

The next episode was even more problematical, with its "action at a distance."

> *After his entry into Capernaum, a centurion came to him, and entreated him. "Sir," he said, "my servant at home is lying ill with paralysis, and is suffering great pain."*
>
> *"I will come and cure him," said Jesus. "Sir," replied the centurion, "I am not a fit person to receive you under my roof: merely say the word, and my servant will be cured. For I myself am also under authority, and have soldiers under me. To one I say 'Go,' and he goes, to another 'Come,' and he comes, and to my slave 'Do this or that,' and he does it." Jesus listened to this reply, and was astonished, and said to the people following him, "I solemnly tell you that in no Israelite have I found faith as great as this. And I tell you that many will come from the east and from the west and will recline at table with Abraham, Isaac and Jacob in the Kingdom of Heaven, while the natural heirs of the Kingdom will be driven out into the darkness outside: there will be the weeping aloud and the gnashing of teeth." And Jesus said to the Centurion, "Go, and just as you have believed, so be it for you." And the servant recovered precisely at that time.*

To Melanie's surprise, and somewhat to her relief, the conversation took a completely different turn. Martha, Roman Catholic by upbringing and one who described herself as "roaming Catholic," spoke of the words of the Mass, "Lord, I am not worthy, only speak the word and my soul shall be healed" which are uttered before the reception of the Holy Communion. "I was surprised to realize where they came from. And how they had changed from the original." Webster, "Parallels" in hand, had this to offer: that in Luke's account of the same episode, the additional information is given, that the centurion "loves our nation and has built us our synagogue," an indication that he was a "godfearer," a Gentile who had become a sympathetic participant in the worship of the local Jewish community.

But perhaps most surprisingly of all was a lengthy discussion about the fact that Jesus lived in a culture built on slavery. Andrew observed indignantly, "He had nothing to say, according to the Gospels, about this. The whole ancient world was built on slavery. Couldn't he have spared a word for them?" Martha recalled that there is a quotation from Isaiah in the sermon at Nazareth. "You remember," she said. "Jesus goes to his home synagogue at Nazareth and reads from Isaiah where it says, among other things, 'He has sent me to proclaim release to the captives . . . ' But that's Luke again," she conceded.

Melanie looked anxiously at her watch, knowing how much remained of the chapter. To expedite matters, she invited Martha's comment on the next section:

> After this Jesus went to the house of Peter, whose mother-in-law he found ill in bed with fever. He touched her hand and the fever left her: and then she rose and waited upon him. In the evening many demoniacs were brought to him, and with a word he expelled the demons; and he cured all the sick, in order that this prediction of the Prophet Isaiah might be fulfilled, "He took on him our weaknesses, and bore the burden of our diseases."

"My Church," said Martha, "claims Peter as the first Bishop of Rome. It is interesting that he was a married man!" But more vehemently, ". . . and look at his poor old mum. No sooner revived, than she is back in the kitchen while the men sit about, talking."

There was discussion about the quote from Isaiah. Someone who knew their Bible, recalled the episode when Jesus, touched by a needy person in a jostling crowd, "felt virtue go out of him." Webster was happy to give the source. "Next week, we will be reading about the women with the hemorrhage. In Mark and Luke, the same episode contains the phrase, '. . . I perceive that power has gone forth from me.' Maybe healing comes at a cost to the healer."

Moving right along, they considered an interlude which seemed out of place, yet perhaps a reflection of the great enthusiasm generated by miraculous actions:

> Seeing great crowds about Him, Jesus had given directions to cross to the other side of the Lake, when a scribe came and said to him, "Teacher, I will follow you wherever you go."
>
> "Foxes have holes," replied Jesus, "and birds have nests; but the Son of Man has nowhere to lay His head."

> *Another of the disciples said to him, "Sir, allow me first to go and bury my father."*
>
> *"Follow me," said Jesus, "and leave the dead to bury their own dead."*

Al complained that the responses Jesus gives in both cases are difficult. "He seems to be exaggerating his homelessness. Presumably, at Capernaum, there would always be a place for him, and at Bethany. Maybe he was feeling a bit lost that day, far from a friendly place. And how harsh it seemed to deny a disciple the opportunity to fulfil the basic duty of a son. If this was all I knew about Jesus," he said, "I wouldn't like him very much!"

It was a good moment to move on!

> *Then he went on board a fishing-boat, and his disciples followed him. But suddenly there arose a great storm on the lake, so that the waves threatened to engulf the boat; but he was asleep. So they came and woke him, crying, "Master, save us, we are drowning!"*
>
> *"Why are you so easily frightened," he replied, "you men of little faith?" Then he rose and reproved the winds and the waves, and there was a perfect calm; and the men, filled with amazement, exclaimed, "What kind of man is this? for the very winds and waves obey him!"*

To spice up the story, Melanie also showed a print of Rembrandt's *Storm on the Sea of Galilee* and reminded them of its dramatic recent history: that it had been stolen from a Boston museum in 1990 and has been missing ever since. "Keep your eyes open at yard sales, there's a big reward!" To her surprise, Andrew knew about this theft. "There's a book I've been reading about famous art robberies. One thing I do remember about this picture is the fact that there are thirteen disciples in the boat and the one looking directly out of the picture is Rembrandt himself. I wonder if he is saying that he considers himself to be a disciple?"

The discussion, however, focussed on the contrast between the disciples ("you men of little faith") and the centurion (" . . . in no Israelite have I found faith as great as this") It seemed that "faith," as a concept, was vague in their minds. Stephen asked, "Would they have shown 'faith' if they had simply sat quietly? Is some kind of passive reliance on God the essence of 'faith'?" No one could give an answer so, as usual, they moved along:

> *On his arrival at the other side, in the country of the Gadarenes, there met him two men possessed by demons, coming from among the tombs: they were so dangerously fierce that no one was able to pass that way. They cried aloud, "What have you to do with us, Son of God? Have you come here to torment us before the time?" Now at some distance from them a vast herd of swine was feeding. So the demons entreated him. "If you drive us out," they said, "send us into the herd of swine."*
>
> *"Go," he replied. Then they came out from the men and went into the swine, whereupon the entire herd instantly rushed down the cliff into the lake and perished in the water. The swineherds fled, and went and told the whole story in the town, including what had happened to the demoniacs. So at once the whole population came out to meet Jesus; and when they saw him, they besought him to leave their country.*

Melanie remarked that there had been previous references to "casting out demons" but that this was the first detailed example. She wondered if the two men were suffering from some form of mental illness, seen at that time as demon possession. Webster recalled reading that this might have been Multiple Personality Disorder. "Sorry to be doing this again," he said, "but in Mark and Luke, Jesus asks 'What is your name?' and the reply is 'Legion, for we are many.'" Al complained, "It's all a bit hard on the pigs and their owners. No wonder Jesus and his disciples were urged to go home."

It had been a long evening. Not for the first time, she regretted her decision to tackle one chapter a week and she groaned inwardly as she realised that twenty chapters lay ahead.

Chapter 9

On Saturday morning, Martha was awakened by her bedside telephone. At first, she didn't recognize the voice. "It's Melanie," said a croaky voice, "and I'm getting this bug that's going around. I'm worried about Tuesday night." The cry for help could scarcely be ignored; Melanie wasn't one who made a fuss for nothing.

Martha hurriedly threw on some clothes and remembered that she had some chicken soup, in her freezer, for such a time as this. Half an hour later, she was at Melanie's bedside, rather shocked by her feverish appearance. "Let me get you something," she said and by the magic of the microwave, she was soon back with soup.

"Here is my special remedy," she said, producing a small bottle of Glenfiddich from her coat pocket. "Purists might be horrified but this is my cure!" Adding a generous pour of the scotch to the hot soup, she persuaded Melanie to try this unlikely combination. The results were almost immediate. Melanie sat up, ready to talk about Tuesday. "I know that I won't be able to go on Tuesday," she croaked. "Please, Martha . . ." There was no way around it, thought Martha and rather reluctantly agreed. She remembered how Al had floundered when he had taken the lead and she didn't want to get into that kind of a fix.

So Tuesday evening came and went and, by Wednesday morning, Melanie was more-or-less herself again, as long as she stayed seated on her sofa. She pretended to work, gazing at the screen of her laptop, checking her emails and generally wishing she were back in bed. Martha's visit was welcome and they sat, side by side, to review the progress of the bug, and to share coffee (and hopefully, not the bug), and an account of Tuesday evening.

Martha began by saying how much the group was enjoying the new regime. "If you are worried that Aunt Matty is looking over your shoulder, then you can forget it. You may not realize that some of us found Matty a bit intimidating; the conversation now is much freer and we don't even need to come with corny jokes!" Melanie was relieved to hear this. "I've wondered about the jokes. They don't come naturally to me and I have hoped that we aren't getting too solemn."

Martha was reassuring. "The jokes, such as they were, covered up a basic nervousness for most of us, I think." Melanie was in a confiding mood. She confessed her frustration: "There is so much in each chapter. We're only scratching the surface."

"Don't forget that this is not a seminar of scholars. It's just us, doing the best we can. What I hear suggests that it is about right. If we want more, there are plenty of places to find it."

Melanie in her systematic way, wanted a blow-by-blow account of the discussion and, she even put up on her lap-top, the text as it had been presented on Tuesday night, beginning with:

> *Accordingly he went on board, and crossing over came to his own town. Here they brought to him a paralytic lying on a bed. Seeing their faith Jesus said to the paralytic, "Take courage, my child; your sins are pardoned."*
>
> *"Such language is impious," said some of the scribes among themselves. Knowing their thoughts Jesus said, "Why are you cherishing evil thoughts in your hearts? Why, which is easier?—to say, 'Your sins are pardoned,' or to say 'Rise up and walk'? But, to prove to you that the Son of Man has authority on earth to pardon sins"—he then says to the paralytic, "Rise, and take up your bed and go home." And he got up, and went off home. And the crowds were awe-struck when they saw it, and ascribed the glory to God who had entrusted such power to a man.*

By Martha's account, Al had wanted to know why there were so many accounts of healings; "Surely, we could have got the idea without so many examples." Stephen had the idea that "the early Church most likely treasured each story and enjoyed hearing them read, Sunday by Sunday. It's like family stories, maybe a bit repetitive to outsiders but special to the family."

Andrew had wondered if this healing story was the same one he had heard in Sunday School: the friends carrying the paralyzed man onto the roof, tearing up the thatch and lowering him down into the place where Jesus was teaching. Webster (who else?) was glad to confirm that Mark and Luke included this detail and wondered if the writer of Matthew's gospel didn't know about it or chose to omit it. "It would be hard to imagine choosing to omit such a fascinating part of the story"

There had been some discussion about "forgiveness of sins," noting that this was the first time in the text for Jesus to say such a thing. They finally agreed that the discussion was mainly directed towards "the Scribes," guardians of the Law who were there to check out what this healer was up to. The logic was discussed: anyone can say "A," anyone can say "B," but when I say "A," the man is healed, therefore when I say "B," his sins must be forgiven. Al, among others, was not impressed with this line of reasoning. "There must be some other logic. But I don't see it."

Melanie interrupted the reportage to ask about Al. "He seems to be a bit negative lately and not so active in the discussions." Martha agreed. "He seems to have other things on his mind."

Back to her report, she confirmed that no one had any doubt that here, at least, Jesus was clearly identifying himself with the "Son of Man." Stephen had been reading ahead and remarked that sometimes Jesus is recorded as speaking of the "Son of Man" as though it were someone else. He looked to the next chapter as an example where Jesus tells his disciples that they won't have finished their missionary journey "before the Son of Man comes." He was eager to share his knowledge that there was a vast scholarly debate over this issue, of whether Jesus claimed to be the "Son of Man". Martha reported her need to rein in his enthusiasm!

She sympathized with Melanie's experience of always needing to watch the clock and push the discussion forward. But the group was growing accustomed to that necessity. So they were happy enough to view:

> Passing on thence Jesus saw a man called Matthew sitting at the tollbooth, and said to him, "Follow me." And he arose, and followed him. And while he was reclining at table, a large number of tax-gathers and notorious sinners were with Jesus and his disciples. The Pharisees noticed this, and they inquired of his disciples, "Why does your Teacher eat with the tax-gatherers and notorious sinners?" He heard the question and replied, "It is not men in good health who require a doctor, but the sick. But go and learn what this means, 'It is mercy that I desire, not sacrifice'; for I did not come to appeal to the righteous, but to sinners."

There was some discussion about the likelihood of Matthew writing this gospel and passing over the decisive event of his life in such a casual fashion. But the main discussion, as Martha remembered it, centered on the table fellowship with "outcasts and sinners" and the beginning of criticism from the Pharisees. Stephen wondered if this episode had implications for excluding anyone from the Eucharist in Sunday worship. "The Church is now a bit more generous in its invitation than it was when I was a boy. Jesus evidently was happy to have at his table anyone at all, disciples or not, virtuous or not." Martha reported that a lively discussion followed with some experience of being included or excluded.

As for the Pharisees, there was knowledge of the hostility that would continue to increase. Inevitably, some of the group had been reading ahead. Melanie remembered her suggestion that they should resist that temptation but she saw now that it was useful to see into later episodes. Martha recounted Stephen again giving a lengthy disquisition on the subject, that the Pharisees were a reform movement within Judaism which emphasized ritual purity as exemplified by hand washing before meals and refusal to share meals with outsiders. He spoke of Chapter 23 of Matthew's gospel where all the hard sayings against the Pharisees are gathered up and wondered again why Jesus had such animosity against them. Andrew wondered if the main point of contention was the elitism, built into the Pharisaic system. He recalled an earlier comment, although he couldn't quite recall who had made it: "If you're a working man, grabbing lunch from a street vendor, there isn't much time and place for handwashing!"

The same would apply to fasting, as the next section would seem to indicate:

> At that time John's disciples came and asked Jesus, "Why do we and the Pharisees fast, but your disciples do not?"
> "Can the bridegroom's party mourn," he replied, "as long as the bridegroom is with them? But other days will come (when the Bridegroom has been taken from them) and then they will fast. No one ever mends an old cloak with a patch of newly woven cloth. Otherwise, the patch put on would tear away some of the old, and a worse hole would be made. Nor do people pour new wine into old wineskins. Otherwise, the skins would split, the wine would escape, and the skins be destroyed. But they put new wine into fresh skins, and both are saved."

Webster was eager to compare this reference to the Bridegroom with the parable in Matthew 25, but, for times sake, Martha held him back. There was some sense that the subsequent section on mending and patching didn't fit very well. It did, however, relate to the perception that the Pharisees were engaged in "mending and patching" when something radically new was needed.

By now, Melanie was feeling a bit groggy again. Martha made her some hot tea and made her comfortable. She was also needing to finish up so that she could get to class and let Melanie sleep. "Three more healings and we were done," she said.

> While he was thus speaking, a ruler came up and profoundly bowing said, "My daughter is just dead; but come and put your hand upon her and she will return to life." And Jesus rose and followed him, as did also his disciples. But a woman who for twelve years had been afflicted with hemorrhage came behind him and touched the tassel of his cloak; for she said to herself, "If I but touch His cloak, I shall be cured." And Jesus turned and saw her, and said, "Take courage, daughter; your faith has cured you." And the woman was restored to health from that moment. Entering the ruler's house, Jesus saw the flute-players and the crowd loudly wailing, and he said, "Go out of the room; the little girl is not dead, but asleep." And they laughed at him. When, however, the place was cleared of the crowd, Jesus went in, and on his taking the little girl by the hand, she rose up. And the report of this spread throughout all that district

Webster reminded them of last weeks discussion about the cost of healing to the healer and the additional detail found in the other gospels ("someone touched me" knowing that power had gone out of him, and the disciples' impatient observation, "of course, someone touched you; we are constantly jostled in this crowd"). Also that the name of the ruler is there recorded: Jairus

Then:

> As Jesus passed on, two blind men followed him, shouting and saying, "Pity us, Son of David." And when he had gone indoors, they came to him. "Do you believe that I can do this?" he asked them. "Yes, Sir," they replied. So he touched their eyes and said, "According to your faith, let it be to you." Then their eyes were opened. And, assuming a stern tone, Jesus said to them, "Be care-

ful to let no one know." But they went out and published his fame in all that district.

Martha took some pleasure in relating that she was able to forestall Webster ("He's sometimes a bit of a pest, isn't he!") by telling the group the fact, surprising to her, that this narrative was a "doublet": that is, it could be twinned with a later healing miracle from Chapter 20. She was even able to show them:

> As they were leaving Jericho, an immense crowd following him, two blind men sitting by the roadside heard that it was Jesus who was passing by, and cried aloud, "Sir, Son of David, pity us." The people angrily tried to silence them, but they cried all the louder. "O Sir, Son of David, pity us," they said.
> So Jesus stood still and called to them. "What shall I do for you?" he asked. "Sir, let our eyes be opened," they replied. Moved with compassion, Jesus touched their eyes, and immediately they regained their sight and followed him.

Many points of similarity but also many differences; on the whole, it was hard to believe that they weren't versions of the same episode. The discussion of why the gospel of Matthew would include both versions was lack-luster and inconclusive. They had had enough for one night. She had displayed the remaining verses of the chapter with a hopeful injunction that they might read for themselves.

> And as they were leaving his presence a dumb demoniac was brought to him. When the demon was expelled, the dumb man could speak. And the crowds exclaimed in astonishment, "Never was such a thing seen in Israel." But the Pharisees maintained, "It is by the power of the Prince of the demons that he drives out the demons."
> And Jesus continued his circuits through all the towns and the villages, teaching in their synagogues and proclaiming the Good News of the Kingdom, and curing every kind of disease and infirmity. And, when he saw the crowds, he was touched with pity for them, because they were distressed and were fainting on the ground like sheep which have no shepherd. Then he said to his disciples, "The harvest is abundant, but the reapers are few; therefore entreat the owner of the harvest to send out reapers into His fields."

It was time for Martha to slip away. She left the remains of the soup and the Glenfiddich in a prominent place and let herself out.

Chapter 10

Melanie had been aware from her childhood that Aunt Matty was a great fan of Albert Schweitzer. Not only did she play recordings of his organ playing but also she often talked about this exemplary man who left behind a brilliant career as a musician and theologian to work as a medical missionary in the Belgian Congo. But it wasn't until she came across an essay about Schweitzer's New Testament work in Aunt Matty's package, that she realized what an important role he played in that field. In particular, she read an excerpt from his autobiography, in which he spoke of studying Matthew Chapter 10 while he was doing army service in 1894. He was struck by verse 23 addressed to the disciples as he sent them out on their missionary journey: "You will not have gone through all the towns of Israel before the Son of Man comes". Schweitzer wrote, "His expectation, however, is not fulfilled. The disciples return without having suffered any persecution . . . The perception dawns on him that the Kingdom of God can only come when he has by suffering and death made atonement . . ." She felt out of her depth, knowing well enough that everything that Schweitzer had written has since been subject to intense debate. She was anxious again about Tuesday.

When they assembled again, she shared some of her thoughts as they contemplated the opening text:

Then he called to him his twelve disciples and gave them authority over evil spirits, to drive them out; and to cure every kind of disease and infirmity. Now the names of the twelve Apostles were these: first, Simon called Peter, and his brother Andrew; James the son of Zebedee, and his brother John; Philip and Bartholomew, Thomas and Matthew the tax-gatherer, James the son of Alphaeus, and Thaddaeus; Simon the Canaanean, and Judas Iscariot, who also betrayed him.

"Do you think," she asked, "that it was a bit like the Prime Minister and his cabinet? Any jostling for position, personal ambition? Did

Jesus ever saw any of them as rivals?" Andrew reminded them of the episode where James and John, sons of Zebedee, sought out positions of power, "to sit on his right hand and on his left in the Kingdom." Webster mentioned that they would encounter this episode in Matthew chapter 20. Al, who sometimes surprised them with his Bible knowledge, said, "Doesn't it say somewhere that Judas 'kept the common purse'? Maybe Minister of Finance in the cabinet of Jesus of Nazareth!"

Before proceeding, Melanie pointed out how obscure some of the apostles were, named in the list, but scarcely mentioned again. "Who knows about Simon the Canaanean, for example?" Al, eager to continue the analogy that, by now, Melanie was coming to regret, replied, "Maybe he went out at the next cabinet shuffle."

She reminded them of the previous week when they had run out of time, so that they hadn't discussed the final verses: ". . . therefore entreat the owner of the harvest to send out reapers into his fields." She wondered if the disciples might have obediently prayed for reapers and discovered, perhaps too late, that they were to be the answers to their own prayers:

> These twelve Jesus sent on a mission, after giving them their instructions: "Go not," he said, "among the Gentiles, and enter no Samaritan town; but, instead of that, go to the lost sheep of Israel's race. And as you go, preach and say, 'The Kingdom of Heaven is close at hand.' Cure the sick, raise the dead to life, cleanse lepers, drive out demons: you have received without payment, give without payment. Provide no gold, nor even silver nor copper to carry in your pockets; no bag for your journey, nor change of linen, nor shoes, nor stick; for the laborer deserves his food. Whatever town or village you enter, inquire for some good man; and make his house your home till you leave the place. When you enter the house, salute it; and if the house deserves it, the peace you invoke shall come upon it. If not, your peace shall return to you. And whoever refuses to receive you or even to listen to your message, as you leave that house or town, shake off the very dust from your feet. I solemnly tell you that it will be more endurable for the land of Sodom and Gomorrah on the Day of Judgement than for that town."

"Maybe," she observed, "they wouldn't have been keen to be chosen if they'd known what was coming! On the one hand, they get power over demons and power to heal, but on the other hand, there they go, totally dependent on the kindness of strangers." Someone murmured, "Or on the kindness of God . . . which might be the same thing."

"But what is the task?" demanded Al. "Just to go about saying, 'The Kingdom of Heaven is close at hand'?" They agreed that "cure the sick, raise the dead to life, cleanse lepers, drive out demons" would speak more eloquently than any sermon. Al seemed sceptical. "We had enough trouble about a person with special powers; now these powers can be passed on to others!" Some of the previous discussion was revisited but without much enlightenment.

Webster took them off in a different direction by noting that Mark's version of this episode allows the disciples to wear sandals! He wondered if Matthew's was earlier; he was bothered by the thought of barefoot apostles wandering the Galilean countryside without even a change of clothing. They tried to visualize a pair of unkempt men arriving at a village, seeking out someone who is "worthy," and making an evaluation of the village's fitness for the Kingdom by the reception they received.

Stephen wondered if the order of the list, given in pairs, might represent the pairings on the journey. "Somewhere Simon the Canaanean is called 'Simon the Zealot', suggesting that he was a member of the movement for violent change. If he and Judas went out together, maybe Judas picked up some of his ideas." Melanie recalled seeing a production of Dorothy Sayers', *The Man Born to be King*, in which Judas seeks to force Jesus to bring in the Kingdom, believing that betrayal to the Romans would precipitate the End. "But I am not so clear what the pairings of the disciples in the list means."

Again it was time to move on and Melanie set before them the next section, remarking that scholarly opinion was almost unanimous that this was reflective of the life of the early church rather than the experience of the disciples:

> "Remember it is I who am sending you out, as sheep into the midst of wolves; prove yourselves as wise as serpents, and as innocent as doves. But beware of men; for they will deliver you up to appear before Sanhedrins, and will flog you in their synagogues; and you will even be put on trial before governors and kings for my sake, to bear witness to them and to the Gentiles. But when they have delivered you up, have no anxiety as to how you shall speak or what you shall say; for at that very time it shall be given you what to say: for it is not you who will speak: it will be the Spirit of your Father speaking through you. Brother will betray

> *brother to death, and father, child; and children will rise against their own parents and will put them to death. And you will be objects of universal hatred because you are called by my name; but he who holds out to the End— he will be saved. Whenever they persecute you in one town, escape to the next; for I solemnly tell you that you will not have gone the round of all the towns of Israel before the Son of Man comes."*

They agreed that such a passage might have been included to show how Jesus, as a prophet, could anticipate the experiences of the next generation. Melanie gave an account of Schweitzer's opinion that Jesus was expecting the Kingdom to be established by heavenly intervention in human affairs within the immediate future. "He seemed to think that Jesus was saying that the missionary tour would not even get completed before it would be interrupted by the coming of the Son of Man." They found this unsatisfactory: why would Matthew include an unfulfilled prophecy or the suggestion that their master was wrong in such a vital matter? Stephen suggested that the statement that they wouldn't finish their missionary journey before the Son of Man came, might simply mean that Jesus would also be continuing his itinerant ministry and would arrive, from time to time, in a village where one of the pairs of disciples had taken up residence.

The discussion returned again to the question of the missionary tour. How would it be organized when six pairs of disciples set out to do the rounds of all the little villages? Did they have maps of the region so that they would be able to divide up the task into six parts? Nothing seemed known about this so they moved on:

> *"The learner is never superior to his teacher, and the servant is never superior to his master. Enough for the learner to be on a level with his teacher, and for the servant to be on a level with his master. If they have called the master of the house Beelzebul, how much more will they slander his servants? Fear them not, however; there is nothing veiled which will not be uncovered, nor secret which will not become known. What I tell you in the dark, speak in the light; and what is whispered into your ear, proclaim upon the roofs of the houses. And do not fear those who kill the body, but cannot kill the soul; but rather fear him who is able to destroy both soul and body in Gehenna."*

They were struck by the continued emphasis on persecution. Some one had looked up "Beelzebul," an ancient way of speaking of an evil being, sometimes translated "Lord of the Flies". This gave rise to a digression to discuss the book by the same name, not a direction which shed any light on the gospel of Matthew. A more fruitful discussion took place about "body" and "soul". Some thought that this was a reminder of the immortality of the soul but others pointed out that the warning was that one should fear rather the one who could destroy both body and soul. Martha had a different proposal. She knew that the word translated as "soul" was the Greek word, *psuche*, often translated "spirit". "Suppose," she said, "that the text is addressed to the whole community of disciples and is giving them confidence that although their bodies might be destroyed, the Spirit which animates the community would continue to be active. The real fear might be the loss of that Spirit if they lose faith and are flung down to the place of burning as those who have lost hope in the Kingdom." Martha conceded that she found traditional ideas of "hell" repulsive. It turned out that she was not alone in this and some expressed gratitude that her explanation gave a reasonable alternative. Webster, in particular, said that her proposal gave him a new freedom from the dark ideas of "hell" which had haunted him all his life. He also wondered if the "him" they were told to fear ("rather fear him who is able to destroy both body and soul in Gehenna") should be seen as Satan who could provoke persecution from opponents and also could cause them to lose hope in the Kingdom.

From this intense discussion, it was with relief that they turned to the comforting verses which followed:

> *"Do not two sparrows sell for a halfpenny? Yet not one of them will fall to the ground without your Father's leave. But as for you, the very hairs on your heads are all numbered. Away then with fear; you are more precious than a multitude of sparrows."*

Stephen had read that translators had various ways of dealing with this, that the original text was "not one of them will fall to the ground without your Father" and that various choices have been made by translators: "not one of them will fall to the ground apart from the will of your Father, without your Father's consent, without your Father's knowing." He liked the idea that in such small events, the Father is there. The discussion took off as they reflected on the way in which humanity had abused the natural order, needing to be reminded that God is in some way present in every event. Eventually Melanie pushed then along to the next section far away from falling sparrows:

> "Every man who acknowledges me before men I also will acknowledge before my Father who is in Heaven. But whoever disowns me before men I also will disown before my Father who is in Heaven."

Now a somber warning, clearly a reference to the Day of Judgement. Webster remarked that there was some irony here, in view of the later failure of the disciples, especially Peter's denials. They wondered when and if Jesus thought of himself in this way, as the one who would have the privileged place before God on that Day. Al needed to have the last word. "What about people like me?" he asked. "I haven't acknowledged him but I haven't denied him, either. I expect that the whole world is full of people in the same boat!" None of them could answer him.

As usual, Melanie interrupted the silence with the sound of the next text being set up:

> "Do not suppose that I came to bring peace to the earth: I did not come to bring peace but a sword. For I came to set a man against his father, a daughter against her mother, and a daughter-in-law against her mother-in-law; and a man's own family will be his foes. Any one who loves father or mother more than me is not worthy of me, and any one who loves son or daughter more than me is not worthy of me; and any one who does not take up his cross and follow where I lead is not worthy of me. To save your life is to lose it, and to lose your life for my sake is to save it."

The conversation centered on the first sentence, one which often has been used to justify various forms of violence. "Maybe," asked Melanie, "Jesus wasn't a pacifist after all?" There was a good deal of discussion as she had hoped. There was sympathy with the view that Jesus was giving fair warning that preaching of the Kingdom would bring opposition, "not peace but a sword" and some incredulity that anyone would see him as a violent revolutionary.

Someone recalled the episode of the Two Swords but wasn't sure of its origin. Webster was glad to direct them to Luke 22 and to read,

> "He said to them, 'When I sent you out with no purse or bag or sandals, did you lack anything?' They said, 'Nothing.' He said to them, 'But now, let him who has a purse take it and likewise a bag. And let him who has no sword sell his mantle and buy one'.... And they said, 'Look, Lord, here are two swords.' And he said to them, 'It is enough.'"

Melanie wasn't eager to encourage discussion of this even though it linked back to the missionary journey they had been discussing. But there was eagerness to come up with the relevant scriptures; some one knew that when Jesus was confronted by the temple police and the others at his arrest, one of the disciples drew a sword and cut off the ear of the servant of the High Priest; there was the additional reminder that Jesus had told that disciple to put away the sword. Another remembered that Jesus had said at that juncture, "All who live by the sword will perish by the sword." Attempts to reconcile these accounts seemed to fail and Webster remarked that this debate had divided the church since the beginning. He slyly suggested that Christian Pacifism would be a good topic for another year, suggesting that Melanie should be making a list of major topics for her future gatherings.

But he went on to point out that the section about conflict within families is a quote from the prophet Micah. He needed to read this as well: *For a son dishonors his father, a daughter rises up against her mother, a daughter-in-law against her mother-in-law; a man's enemies are members of his own household.*

He wondered why the familiar formula "... that the words of the Prophet might be fulfilled ..." was omitted.

Melanie knew their signs of weariness and once again used her leadership power to bring their gathering to an end. She sent them off with advice to re-read the final verses of Chapter 10 and to be ready for Chapter 11

As they packed up their belongings, the screen showed the final verses:

> "Whoever receives you receives me, and whoever receives me receives Him who sent me. Every one who receives a prophet, because he is a prophet, will receive a prophet's reward, and every one who receives a righteous man, because he is a righteous man, will receive a righteous man's reward. And whoever gives one of these little ones even a cup of cold water to drink because he is a disciple, I solemnly tell you that he will not lose his reward."

Chapter 11

WEBSTER WAS SURPRISED TO receive a call from Melanie. She explained that she was under great pressure. "Most of the time, I enjoy my work. But we are now preparing for the 'lawsuit from hell'. We will all be working sixteen-hour days. I am wondering if you would be willing to lead on Tuesday. I won't have a moment to prepare. I doubt if I'll even be there." Webster was surprised that she would ask him as he had sensed that he didn't always make her leadership easy with his frequent interjections. However he didn't hesitate. "I'll do my best to fill your shoes. It won't be easy."

When Webster arrived the following Tuesday, he was surprised that Melanie had, after all, been able to attend. "Things moved faster than I expected," she said, "but don't think that you're off the hook. I haven't had a moment even to read the text."

Her presence made the transition easier and she explained her predicament and turned the "chair" over to Webster. "Please," he begged, "don't let me turn this into a lecture. Interrupt early and often. After all, that's what I do!" Then to the first section, a single verse:

> When Jesus had concluded his instructions to his twelve disciples, he left in order to teach and to proclaim his message in the neighboring towns.

He suggested that this was really the last verse of the previous chapter and commented that it was relevant to their previous discussion; "Remember," he said, "the text about the disciples not finishing their missionary tour before the Son of Man came. One possibility was that he meant nothing more than a meeting with them on their way. This verse would support that idea." They showed no great interest in revisiting that discussion so the next section was displayed:

> *Now John had heard in prison about the Christ's doings, and he sent some of his disciples to inquire: "Are you the Coming One, or is it a different person that we are to expect?"*
>
> *"Go and report to John what you see and hear," replied Jesus; "blind eyes receive sight, and cripples walk; lepers are cleansed, and deaf ears hear; the dead are raised to life, and the poor have the Good News proclaimed to them; and blessed is every one who does not stumble and fall because of my claims."*

"Do you remember our earlier session and the discussion about John the Baptist?" asked Webster. "A month from now we'll be in Matthew 14 where his martyrdom is described." They wondered if imprisonment had led to a failure of nerve on the part of John or perhaps impatience that Jesus was so slow in bringing in the Kingdom. Stephen remarked that questions directed to Jesus didn't get a simple answer. "Is it like questions addressed to public figures today?" He wondered whether this was and is a form of evasiveness or simply a way of putting a question into a broader context. Others contested the word "evasiveness" and thought that a simple affirmative answer would scarcely be reassuring to the imprisoned John. Andrew suggested, "The answer actually given would make clear that Jesus wasn't just sitting in Nazareth, waiting for something to happen but was, in fact, out fulfilling his destiny as Messiah. Encoded into the response was a blessing on John if he holds fast to his conviction which appears to have been wavering." Moving on, they considered:

> *When the messengers had taken their leave, Jesus proceeded to say to the multitude concerning John, "What did you go out into the desert to gaze at? A reed waving in the wind? But what did you go out to see? A man luxuriously dressed? Those who wear luxurious clothes are to be found in kings' palaces. But why did you go out? To see a prophet? Yes, I tell you, and far more than a prophet. This is he of whom it is written, 'See I am sending My messenger before Thy face, and he will make Thy road ready before Thee.'*
>
> *I solemnly tell you that among all of woman born no greater has ever been raised up than John the Baptist; yet one who is least in the Kingdom of Heaven is greater than he."*

Al was eager to leap in. He expressed himself strongly; "Just when I was getting to like Jesus again, he throws out a comment like this! First, he praises John as prophet and the greatest of all born to women, then in the next breath, he gives him a failing grade!" This provoked the usual response. Some wondered if this evaluation of John had been inserted into the text by those in the early church who worried that the community of John's disciples were becoming a serious problem. Andrew thought that it was a rhetorical way of making the strongest possible distinction between the old and the new. "The Kingdom was to be so radical that its most distinguished forerunners were less than its humblest citizens." Al was scarcely placated. He recalled his earlier complaint that Jesus wouldn't let prospective disciples bury a dead father or say goodbye to family members. "It all leaves me with a bad taste in my mouth!" he grumbled.

Webster needed to move the discussion forward, especially as the next section was a tough nut to crack:

> "But from the time of John the Baptist till now, the Kingdom of Heaven has been suffering violent assault, and the violent have been seizing it by force. For all the Prophets and the Law taught until John. And (if you are willing to receive it) he is the Elijah who was to come. Listen, every one who has ears!"

Webster warned all present that this text was regarded by almost everyone as problematic. Who was being referred to as perpetrating violence upon the Kingdom? One traditional interpretation was outlined by Webster: that the "time of John the Baptist" was a shorthand way of referring to the time of the prophets, approximately the centuries during which the prophets of the Old Testament were active. During that time, "the Kingdom" was almost always under attack by its neighbors. But an objection to that point of view was soon apparent: that according to tradition, the prophetic voice had been silent for several hundred years and a description of those ancient times as the "time of John the Baptist" seemed a stretch. Stephen wondered about the disciple, Simon the Canaanean who was also known as Simon the Zealot. "Could he have tried to introduce the violent methods of the Zealots into the preaching of the Kingdom? Maybe in some way heading up a break-away movement?" They agreed that no obvious solution was at hand and Webster assured them that the scholars had been debating this text since the beginning.

They moved on to examine the notion that John the Baptist was Elijah come back to earth. Webster reminded them that Elijah was "taken up to heaven in a whirlwind" according to Second Kings 2 and Al wanted to know if this meant that Christians believed in re-incarnation! More puzzling was the notion that John was Elijah "if you are willing to believe it." Webster said, "It's a complete muddle. In John's Gospel, chapter 1, John is denying that he is Elijah. But when we get to Matthew chapter 17, we will find Jesus saying, 'Elijah has indeed come . . . ' and that when he said that, it dawned on the disciples that he was speaking about John the Baptist." Webster was willing to leave it at that, proposing the tentative solution that the perception that John the Baptist was Elijah was subjective. Not everyone was satisfied but no one seemed inclined to pursue the matter. So they went on:

> "But to what shall I compare the present generation? It is like children sitting in the open places, who call to their playmates. 'We have played the flute to you,' they say, 'and you have not danced: we have sung dirges, and you have not beaten your breasts.' For John came neither eating nor drinking, and they say, 'He has a demon.' The Son of Man came eating and drinking, and they exclaim, 'See this man! —given to gluttony and tippling, and a friend of tax-gatherers and notorious sinners!' And yet wisdom is vindicated by her actions."

They all seemed to recognize the reference to children playing at weddings and funerals and the comparison made of the austerities preached by John the Baptist, on the one hand, and the scandalous freedoms which Jesus and his disciples enjoyed, on the other. Webster reminded them that the life to which Jesus called people was not a life of self-denial but celebration of new freedoms. He recalled Matthew chapter 9: "the days will come when the Bridegroom is taken away, then they will fast". Stephen wondered if modern Christians should re-discover fasting as a spiritual discipline. There seemed to be a lack of enthusiasm for this idea but there was a discussion about the idea that Christians might not be surprised if they feel a sense of loss and even melancholy! If the early Christians were sustained by an expectation that their Lord would soon return, what sustains modern Christians? Al had something to say on this matter. "There are many Christians who are sustained by exactly the same belief. I have plenty of *Left Behind* books, 'left behind' in my bookstore. As far as I can make out, they are based on ideas gleaned from prophetic parts of the Bible, now applied to the twenty first century." He acknowledged that such ideas were controversial with a substantial history of others over the centuries who had tried to predict the coming of the Kingdom. "And how," asked Webster, "is wisdom vindicated by her actions?" As a general piece of common sense, they had no trouble with this but found it hard to fit into the context.

Webster had learned from Melanie that "if in doubt, move along," so he did! They read the next section from the screen:

> *Then he began to upbraid the towns where most of his mighty works had been done—because they had not repented. "Alas for thee, Chorazin!" he cried. "Alas for thee, Bethsaida! For had the mighty works been done in Tyre and Sidon which have been done in both of you, they would long ago have repented, covered with sackcloth and ashes. Only I tell you that it will be more endurable for Tyre and Sidon on the day of Judgement than for you. And thou, Capernaum, shalt thou be exalted even to Heaven? Even to Hades you shall descend. For had the mighty works been done in Sodom which have been done in thee, it would have remained until now. Only I tell you all, that it will be more endurable for the land of Sodom on the day of Judgement than for thee."*

Webster remarked that the "lament" is a classic literary form in the prophetic writings and that this fits into that tradition. He reminded them of a similar passage in Chapter 10 where Sodom and Gomorrah were the cities with better chances than those towns that rejected the Kingdom message. "Sodom and Gomorrah were bywords for moral corruption, Tyre and Sidon represented dangerous enemies, centers of Philistine power. I wonder why Capernaum is singled out for special mention. Perhaps because later on Jesus is rejected in no uncertain terms at Capernaum and gives the famous opinion that a prophet is not without honor except in his own country."

Melanie saw how easily Webster was allowing the session to become a monologue and she was even more uneasy with the willingness the group had to allow this to happen. But she couldn't think of an intervention and was glad when they tackled the next section:

> *About that time Jesus exclaimed, "I heartily praise Thee, Father, Lord of Heaven and of earth, that Thou hast hidden these things*

> *from the wise and men of discernment, and hast unveiled them to babes. Yes, Father, for such has been Thy gracious will. All things have been handed over to me by my Father, and no one fully knows the Son except the Father, nor does any one fully know the Father except the Son and all to whom the Son chooses to reveal Him."*

Now Webster was in his element. He explained the theory that those parts of Matthew and Luke which were identical but didn't appear in Mark had given rise to the hypothetical document known as Q. He was ready enough to explain that Q stood for "Quelle," a German word for "source" and Melanie braced herself for a lecture of the history of the "Synoptic Problem". She was relieved that he hadn't come ready to show what Q might have looked like but contented himself with the observation that the text on the screen was a part of Q. Then he surprised her by asking a question, " What does this text remind you of?" There was a silence as he tried to nudge them along to the right answer and eventually someone who had done their homework said, "John's Gospel". Melanie felt a bit ashamed in begrudging Webster his evident pleasure at having a smart student in the class! He didn't give rewards for this right answer but spoke of the description given long ago, that the text was "a Johannine thunderbolt" Al wanted to know why it deserved such a description and Webster floundered a bit. "I suppose," he said, "because it describes a relation between Son and Father that isn't a usual style of expression in Matthew." Al wasn't to be put off. "It's a kind of a prayer, isn't it? Are we to imagine Jesus saying this out loud and in public? Or did someone compose it later on?" As usual, no one could answer him and they moved along to a favorite passage,

> *"Come to me, all you toiling and burdened ones, and I will give you rest. Take my yoke upon you and learn from me; for I am gentle and lowly in heart, and you will find rest for your souls. For it is good to bear my yoke, and my burden is light."*

The imagery of the yoke attracted some discussion. Webster was quick to point out that the yoke was the method of allowing two animals to share the work; he wondered if the main point of the imagery was that the disciples weren't to take on the whole burden alone but in pairs, as during their missionary tour. Another possibility was voiced: that the invitation was to see ourselves "yoked" to Jesus himself. But against that was the repeated promise of "rest" rather than shared labor. It seemed that Jesus was promising his disciples an easy time. This seemed at odds with what they had read in Matthew 10 in which Jesus asks his disciples to take up the cross. "Maybe earlier on, Jesus wishes to encourage his disciples and then later comes to understand that his own sufferings would involve them as well," said Stephen and that brought the evening to an end.

As she left, Melanie felt a restored confidence that, whatever limitations she brought to the unsought task, at least her style encouraged discussion!

Chapter 12

They sat again in the same coffee shop but now just Al and Melanie, meeting at his request. She teased him about the previous time when they met with Webster and the "Sprite" stunt. He had the grace to look sheepish and to agree that he preferred coffee. "I was younger at the time," he offered by way of defense, "and rather inclined to show off!"

Their conversation became more serious as he revealed his reaction to the Tuesday evenings.

"I'm beginning to understand why people get hooked. There's something about this story which won't let go." Melanie was somewhat uncertain of where this was leading and why he would be telling her this. Was this his way of telling her of some religious experience? He continued, "In my business, I read a lot of books and I've been a reader all my life but I can't think of another experience quite like this. I am thinking that there are millions of people around the world who have been caught up by this story." She was still uneasy about the direction their conversation was taking. She tried a different tack; " Do you think that you will give church-going a second look?" He sighed and sipped his coffee. "That's a very different question. You may not know that I was brought up in a home where my mother was very angry with the church and I guess that I still carry some of that with me. And, have you noticed that with all the advice given by Jesus to his disciples and to others, he says never a word about being regular at synagogue?" She wondered if one could argue from silence; maybe it was so ingrained that they didn't need reminding. Al recalled an earlier discussion. "Remember when I took over for an evening, when Webster surprised me with his knowledge that Jesus moved out of Nazareth for a good reason. That the synagogue had become too hot to hold him. I looked up that reference and discovered that he went to the synagogue 'as was his custom.' " She thought about this for a moment. "I wonder," she asked, "if the experience at Nazareth soured him on synagogue attendance from then on?"

She suddenly had an idea that went back to Aunt Matty. "From time to time," she said, "Aunt Matty would send me pieces she had read and I would file them away, sometimes without reading them. This one piece from Schweitzer might interest you." She opened up her laptop and found the folder and file she needed. "Take a look," she invited, turning the screen in his direction. He read aloud:

> He comes to us as one unknown, without a name, as of old by the lakeside, he came to those men who knew him not. He speaks to us the same words, "Follow thou me" and sets us to the tasks which he has to fulfill for our time. He commands and to those who obey him, whether they be wise or simple, he will reveal himself in the toils, the conflicts, the sufferings which they shall pass through in his fellowship, and, as an ineffable mystery, they shall learn in their own experience, who he is.

"Whoa!" he exclaimed, "this is something!" She agreed. "Maybe it's a starting place." He asked for a copy and she promised to attach a copy to an email. "It is the last paragraph of Schweitzer's famous book, 'The Quest for the Historical Jesus' and represents his conclusion after he had examined all the opinions of his day. Maybe a Christian isn't so much a person who believes certain things but a person who consciously sets out to respond to a certain kind of call."

"And then, in responding, comes to believe," she silently wondered.

So their conversation ended; at least, it turned to more mundane topics and they finished their coffees and went their separate ways.

Melanie and Al both thought about Schweitzer's words in the following days, each wondering how life would be if such words were taken seriously; each, unknown to the other, arriving at the place of Eliot's Magi, "no longer at ease in the old dispensation."

But life went on, the law office and the bookstore keeping them busy. By Tuesday, Melanie was ready and energized to tackle Chapter 12, seeing the halfway point not so far off. As she read, she perceived a change, a hardening of attitudes towards Jesus. This seemed believable since Jesus evidently did not go out of his way to ingratiate himself. She had read some of Matty's notes about the Jesus Seminar which seemed content with Jesus as a teacher of wisdom; scarcely one who would provoke such opposition and end up on a cross!

So came Tuesday and another encounter with Matthew:

> *About that time Jesus passed on the Sabbath through the wheat fields; and his disciples became hungry, and began to gather ears of wheat and eat them. But the Pharisees saw it and said to him, "Look! Your disciples are doing what the Law forbids them to do on the Sabbath."*
>
> *"Have you never read," he replied, "what David did when he and his men were hungry? how he entered the House of God and ate the presented loaves, which it was not lawful for him or his men to eat, nor for any except the priests? And have you not read in the Law how on the Sabbath the priests in the Temple break the Sabbath without incurring guilt? But I tell you that there is here that which is greater than the Temple. And if you knew what this means, 'It is mercy I desire, not sacrifice', you would not have condemned those who are without guilt. For the Son of Man is the Lord of the Sabbath."*

They all seemed to have tracked down the story from First Samuel where David and his band of outlaws receive the consecrated bread from the priest. Al, in his usual way, complained that whatever David did, it wasn't clear that he did it on the Sabbath and that, in any case, the priest who gave the holy bread was more likely to incur blame than those who received it. "On the other hand," countered Stephen, "maybe the point of this isn't Sabbath keeping but rather the need for humane considerations to have higher place than legal requirements." Al seemed unconvinced. "If David and his men and the disciples of Jesus had been starving and at the point of death, I could go along with that . . ."

They were accustomed to reaching such moments when further discussion might be unprofitable so Melanie moved them along to the next argument: that priests working on the Sabbath legitimized what the disciples were doing. More objections were voiced: that the Law specifically gave permission to the priests to "break the Sabbath": was it then clear that this would give permission for non-priests like the disciples to act as they did?

Melanie saw that the continuing line of argument: "mercy not sacrifice": would continue this discussion in the same way and she directed their attention to the last sentence, that the Son of Man is Lord of the Sabbath. She wondered if this was the first step to the abolition of Sabbath-keeping. The older members of the group recalled days when

Christians regarded avoidance of work on Sunday as a primary duty and how that had, in their memory, become avoidance of any enjoyment. Toys put away, Sunday sports seen as sinful and so on. Not great memories and a good time to move along!

> *Departing thence he went to their synagogue, where there was a man with a shriveled hand. And they questioned him, "Is it right to cure people on the Sabbath?" Their intention was to bring a charge against him. "Which of you is there," he replied, "who, if he has but a single sheep and it falls into a ditch on the Sabbath, will not lay hold of it and lift it out? Is not a man, however, far superior to a sheep? Therefore it is right to do good on the Sabbath." Then he said to the man, "Stretch out your hand." And he stretched it out, and it was restored quite sound like the other.*

Clearly this was a continuation, in action, of the same arguments, previously conducted in words. And with the same objections: the sheep in the ditch might be an easy prey for predators if left overnight in the ditch. But the man with the shriveled hand might easily have waited another day and then received healing. Melanie was taken somewhat by surprise when Al said, "There is something going on here that I don't understand. Maybe Jesus is being deliberately provocative!"

Stephen made a humorous comment, unusual for him! "I suppose," he said, "that the man, asked to 'stretch out your hand', instinctively stretched out his good arm. 'No, no, the other one,' says Jesus and there he was, cured. But the opponents could only stretch out a fist! "

And this gave the opportunity to lead into the first note of lethal intent from the opponents, seemingly a disproportionate response:

> *But the Pharisees after leaving the synagogue consulted together against him, how they might destroy him. Aware of this, Jesus departed elsewhere; and a great number of people followed him, all of whom he cured. But he gave them strict injunctions not to publicize his doings, that those words of the prophet Isaiah might be fulfilled, "This is My servant whom I have chosen, My dearly loved One in whom My soul takes pleasure. I will put My spirit upon Him, and He will announce justice to the nations. He will not wrangle or raise His voice, nor will His voice be heard in the broad ways. A crushed reed He will not utterly break, nor will He quench the still smoldering wick, until He has led on justice to victory. And on His name shall the nations rest their hopes."*

They wondered about the response of the Pharisees; were they really ready for murder? Webster, who had thought about this during the week, had discovered that the word translated "destroy," could also mean, "put out of the way" and he found it more plausible that their intention was to do exactly that.

Martha, so often quiet, wondered out loud about the choice of this long passage from Isaiah. "Are we to believe from this that Jesus was the 'gentle Jesus, meek and mild' from the hymn? He seemed happy to engage in controversy with his opponents and his voice 'was heard in the broad ways' constantly as far as we can understand the story to date." Again someone suggested that the "broad ways" referred to the Roman highways and that one could argue that Jesus restricted himself to the paths and tracks which went from village to village. Andrew was quite eloquent on this. "I understand that the 'crushed reed' and the 'smoldering wick' might represent objects of little or no value, likely to be discarded. Perhaps Jesus saw value where no one else would see it, in crushed hopes and almost extinguished dreams."

Melanie was inclined to leave it at that, feeling that Andrew had said something rather memorable. And so, on they went:

> At that time a demoniac was brought to him, blind and dumb; and he cured him, so that the dumb man could speak and see. And the crowds of people were all filled with amazement and said, "Can this be the Son of David?" The Pharisees heard it and said, "This man only expels demons by the power of Beelzebul, the Prince of demons." Knowing their thoughts, he said to them, "Every kingdom, in which civil war has raged, suffers desolation; and every city or house in which there is internal strife will be brought low. And if Satan is expelling Satan, he has begun to make war on himself: how therefore shall his kingdom last? And if it is by Beelzebul's power that I expel the demons, by whose power do your disciples expel them? They therefore shall be your judges. But if it is by the power of the Spirit of God that I expel the demons, it is evident that the Kingdom of God has come upon you. Again, how can any one enter the house of a strong man and carry off his goods, unless first of all he masters and secures the strong man: then he will ransack his house."

Melanie reminded them that this attack was briefly mentioned in Chapter 9 in which his opponents claimed that "it was by the Prince of demons he drove out demons," and that in Chapter 10, in his missionary discourse, Jesus is reported to have said the disciples would endure the same attacks: "If the head of the household is called Beelzebul, how much more the members of the household." Here the defense is offered. It didn't satisfy Stephen who suggested that civil war among the powers of the "Dark Side" might be not so surprising; moreover, that the question, "How shall his kingdom last?" might be countered by the thought that "his kingdom" was about to be overthrown by the establishment of the Kingdom of God. Melanie worried that both Al and Stephen were becoming analytical in a way that wasn't entirely helpful. She wondered if they were missing the point but she would have been hard pressed to say exactly what the point was!

Webster pushed the discussion in another direction. He asked about the question, "... by whom do your disciples cast them out?" He wanted to know whether exorcism was a common practice or whether Jesus was being ironic, saying something like "you know that casting out demons is something your disciples try and that they have no success; supposing they were successful. Would you accuse them also being in league with Beelzebul?" Nobody thought much of his attempt to re-interpret the words of the text but there were plenty of thoughts about exorcism. It struck Melanie as strange that previous references to the subject hadn't given rise to much discussion but there were comments about the fascination with exorcism in movies and books, mention of exorcism in the Roman Catholic Church and in the early church. Martha, who had spent time in Africa, could relate an eyewitness account of a village exorcist at work. It was unclear that this discussion shed much light on the text but it was a reminder that in a great part of the world, the belief in evil powers was alive and well.

Time to move on!

> "The man who is not with me is against me, and he who is not gathering with me is scattering abroad. This is why I tell you that men may find forgiveness for every other sin and impious word, but that for impious speaking against the Holy Spirit they shall find no forgiveness. And whoever shall speak against the Son of Man may obtain forgiveness; but whoever speaks against the Holy Spirit, neither in this nor in the coming age shall he obtain forgiveness."

The first sentence caused considerable discussion. Did it mean that everyone who was not committed as a disciple of Jesus was seen as an opponent? And should Christians view the world today in such a fashion? To complicate matters, Webster had discovered the text in Mark and Luke which took a very different tack: John says, "Master, we saw a man driving out demons in your name and we tried to stop him because he is not one of us." And Jesus replies, "Do not stop him for whoever is not against you is for you." Al thought that this more liberal attitude might represent a later understanding in the life of Jesus. But he was also eager to proceed to the next part of the text; to discuss the idea of unforgivable sin. "This is a problem for me," he said. "I can't see why speaking against the Holy Spirit should be so unforgivable." He paused, not quite finished. "I remember that we had similar trouble over the saying in the Sermon on the Mount about calling your brother a fool, with the threat of being thrown down into Gehenna." There was some confused discussion based on ideas learned elsewhere that identified "the unforgivable sin" is suicide or, possibly, despair. Melanie pointed out that the context of what the Pharisees were saying had to be factored into the discussion: the unforgivable sin seemed to be an unwillingness to recognize the works of the Kingdom. "Do those who deliberately adopt such a view put themselves outside the possibility of forgiveness? What happens if we think evil to that which is good?" She spoke with some pain about a couple whom she knew whose marriage was irredeemably broken. Any offer of forgiveness was always interpreted as an attempt to manipulate the situation and so there was something like "unforgivable sin" at work. Not everyone was buying her theory and she wasn't satisfied with it herself but it was the best she could do.

> *"Either grant the tree to be wholesome and its fruit wholesome, or the tree poisonous and its fruit poisonous; for the tree is known by its fruit. O vipers' brood, how can you speak what is good when you are evil? For it is from the overflow of the heart that the mouth speaks. A good man from his good store produces good things, and a bad man from his bad store produces bad things. But I tell you that for every careless word that men shall speak they will be held accountable on the day of Judgement. For each of you by your words shall be justified, or by your words shall be condemned."*

The previous argument was made even more contentious when the "careless word" was put into the mix. If this was the true teaching of the Kingdom, who could hope for mercy? Al was outraged. "What's going on?" he asked. "First, the prospective penalty for calling your brother a fool, then an irreversible penalty for speaking against the Holy Spirit and now, every careless word. There will be long lineups on Judgement Day! Most of the utterances of my whole life have been 'careless words'! Am I to be condemned by careless words?" There was sympathy for his indignation but Stephen suggested that the last sentence might be an interpolation; he observed the change of tense from "they" in the preceding verse to "you" in the last verse. "Could it be," he wondered, "that the reference at the end might not be to 'careless words' but to words uttered perhaps at baptism or in a time of persecution?" There was some support for this although they agreed that its meaning might remain obscure. Some one mentioned the baptismal formula quoted by St. Paul: "confess with the mouth and believe in the heart . . ."

Melanie was conscious of the time remaining and obtained agreement that they should limit discussion as severely as possible. For the next section, they would only consider the "sign of Jonah":

> *Then he was accosted by some of the Scribes and of the Pharisees who said, "Teacher, we wish to see a sign given by you."*
>
> *"Wicked and faithless generation!" he replied. "They clamor for a sign, but none shall be given to them except the sign of the Prophet Jonah. For just as Jonah was three days and three nights in the sea-monster's belly, so will the Son of Man be three days and three nights in the heart of the earth. There will stand up men of Nineveh at the judgement together with the present generation, and will condemn it; because they repented at the preaching of Jonah, and consider this: there is one greater than Jonah here. The Queen of the South will awake at the judgement together with the present generation, and will condemn it; because she came from the ends of the earth to hear the wisdom of Solomon, and consider this: there is one greater than Solomon here."*

They agreed that the reference was to the death and resurrection of Jesus, remarking that this was the first time that such a prospect was mentioned. The problem of "three days and three nights" was raised with the observation that Friday afternoon until Sunday morning would scarcely fulfil that prediction. Webster threw in a theory he had encountered: that the crucifixion took place on a Thursday! He commented that the evidence seemed ambiguous and that there was some special pleading to preserve the exact truth of the prediction.

They then went on to consider the remaining sections, the first of which seemed to be related to the earlier part of the chapter and was evidently a warning about the possible dangers of exorcism:

> *"No sooner however has the foul spirit gone out of the man, then he roams about in places where there is no water, seeking rest but finding none. Then he says, 'I will return to my house that I left;' and he comes and finds it unoccupied, swept clean, and in good order. Then he goes and brings back with him seven other spirits more wicked than himself, and they come in and dwell there; and in the end that man's condition becomes worse than it was at first. So will it be also with the present wicked generation."*

And the second, which, had time been available might have stimulated a discussion about the strained relations between Jesus and his family:

> *While he was still addressing the people his mother and his brothers were standing on the edge of the crowd desiring to speak to him. So some one told him, "Your mother and your brothers are standing outside, and desire to speak to you."*
>
> *"Who is my mother?" he said to the man; "and who are my brothers?" And pointing to his disciples he added, "See here are my mother and my brothers. To obey my Father who is in Heaven—that is to be my brother and my sister and my mother."*

But they were now exhausted and decided to call it a day!

Chapter 13

It had been Matty's custom to have her group around to the house on the Tuesday before Christmas for Yuletide cheer and the singing of carols. Those events were remembered well by Melanie who had generally made herself scarce, especially for the carols. She had never developed a taste for carols. She recalled her complaint when still a child: "What does it mean, 'the little Lord Jesus no crying he makes'. Is it because he is the perfect baby and perfect babies don't cry?" And later, as a teenager, she complained about "Sing of Mary, pure and lowly, virgin mother, undefiled," which she had heard at a Christmas service. She recalled the Christmas morning argument about whether having sex could be equated to defilement; it hadn't been one of the greatest Christmas mornings on record!

It certainly wasn't part of her legacy to continue Matty's tradition, no doubt in her mind about that! It would be business as usual. And that would be fine because the next chapter was full of parables concerning which she had come across another writing by Jeremias who had helped her through the Lord's Prayer. This time a small book, "The Parables of Jesus" which she found challenging (since she could scarcely read any Greek) but convincing. She was particularly impressed by the argument of Jeremias about the interpretation of the parables of the Sower and the Wheat and the Darnel and tried to get the basics in her head so that she could explain these ideas to the group.

It was quite a surprise, however, when she arrived at the Parish House the next Tuesday, to find that a small Christmas celebration had been arranged: some rather palatable hot rum toddy and various seasonal nibbles. Even more surprising were some expressions of appreciation for her leadership and a toast proposed by Webster supported with evident enthusiasm by all present. And no carols!

Eventually, they were willing to fill their glasses one last time and bring them to their usual places around the table. "Well," she said, "thanks to one and all. Quite up to Matty's standards!"

With time taken for these festivities, she observed that they would not get through the whole chapter and she wanted to get started with the parable of the Sower:

> *That same day Jesus had left the house and was sitting on the shore of the Lake, when a vast multitude of people crowded round him. He therefore went on board a boat and sat there, while all the people stood on the shore. He then spoke many things to them in parables. "The sower goes out," he said, "to sow. As he sows, some of the seed falls by the wayside, and the birds come and peck it up. Some falls on rocky ground, where it has but scanty soil. It quickly shows itself above ground, because it has no depth of earth; but when the sun is risen, it is scorched by the heat, and, through having no root, it withers up. Some fall among the thorns; but the thorns spring up and stifle them. But a portion falls upon good ground, and gives a return, some a hundred for one, some sixty, some thirty. Listen, every one who has ears!"*
>
> *And his disciples came and asked him, "Why do you speak to them in parables?"*
>
> *"Because," he replied, "while to you it is granted to know the secrets of the Kingdom of Heaven, to them it is not. For whoever has, to him more shall be given, and he shall have abundance; but whoever has not, from him even what he has shall be taken away. I speak to them in parables for this reason, that while looking they do not see, and while hearing they neither hear nor understand. And in regard to them the prophecy of Isaiah is receiving fulfillment: 'You will hear and hear and by no means understand, and you will look and look and by no means see. For this people's mind is stupefied, their hearing has become dull, and their eyes, they have closed; to prevent their ever seeing with their eyes, or hearing with their ears, or understanding with their minds, and turning back, so that I might heal them.' But as for you, blessed are your eyes, for they see, and your ears, for they hear. For I solemnly tell you that many prophets and holy men have longed to see the sights*

you see, and have not seen them, and to hear the words you hear, and have not heard them.

To you then I will explain the parable of the Sower. When a man hears the word concerning the Kingdom and does not understand it, the Evil one comes and catches away what has been sown in his heart. This is he who has received the seed by the roadside. He who has received the seed on the rocky ground is the man who hears the word and immediately receives it with joy. It has struck no root, however, within him. He continues for a time, but when suffering comes, or persecution, because of the message, he at once stumbles and falls. He who has received the seed among the thorns is the man who hears the word, but the cares of the present age and the delusions of riches quite stifle the word, and it becomes unfruitful. But he who has received the seed on good ground is he who hears and understands. Such hearers give a return, and yield one a hundred for one, another sixty, another thirty."

She displayed this lengthy passage and set out to summarize the argument she had read concerning the interpretation. She quoted Jeremias, "I had long held out against the conclusion that the interpretation must be ascribed to the primitive Church . . . but it is unavoidable." They listened as she haltingly explained the argument: that there were too many words used in the interpretation which were not used elsewhere in Matthew. She took as an example "ho logos" (the word) which appears five times. She also mentioned the Gospel of Thomas which most of them had heard about, one of the writings that had not been included in our Bible but had some claim to authenticity. "In that Gospel the parable is given but not the interpretation. Jeremias regards this as an indication that the parable existed independently at one time."

They listened politely but did not seem convinced, perhaps because they had heard too many sermons on the Parable of the Sower and were wedded to the traditional explanation. "If we follow the argument of Jeremias," asked Webster, "what does the parable mean?" Melanie was able to summarize what she had read: that as the sower experiences many frustrations and disappointments in his work but is eventually rewarded by a bountiful harvest, so the labor of proclaiming the Kingdom, with its similar frustrations and disappointments, will lead to a triumphant end. Al remarked that he couldn't see why only one interpretation needed to be received. "Surely both are possible and maybe others. Isn't that part of the idea of parables?" Martha wondered how the first hearers would react. "It seems to me that they would be surprised at reckless behavior. Seed grain was precious and here the sower flings it about without thought. No wonder much of it came to a bad end. Maybe the lesson of the parable is to be found in the reckless generosity of the sower and, by extension, the reckless generosity of God."

There was some strong support for this but the discussion was pushed ahead by Al who wanted to get opinions about the quote from Isaiah. "It sounds to me," he said, "as if the parables were chosen to make it impossible for outsiders to get into the Kingdom. The word 'prevent' seems so problematic!" Stephen was able to help. He had experienced the same feeling and had looked up other translations. "They do give a variety of possibilities," he reported. "For example, the New International Version has 'For this people's heart has become callused; they hardly hear with their ears and they have closed their eyes. Otherwise they might see with their eyes, hear with their ears, understand with their hearts and turn, and I would heal them.' This changes the tone considerably, I think." Al agreed and said that he needed to be reminded that they were reading a translation. He was surprised that the same text could give such different readings.

Melanie moved them along but warned them that she had rearranged the text so that the next parable, the Parable of the Wheat and the Darnel, and its interpretation were consecutive. "In the original, another parable is placed between and I thought it useful to make this rearrangement." They could scarcely protest since there it was on the screen:

> *Another parable he put before them. "The Kingdom of Heaven," he said, "may be compared to a man who has sown good seed in his field, but during the night his enemy comes, and over the first seed he sows darnel among the wheat, and goes away. But when the blade shoots up and the grain is formed, then appears the darnel also. So the farmer's men come and ask him, 'Sir, was it not good seed that you sowed on your land? Where then does the darnel come from?' 'Some enemy has done this,' he said. 'Shall we go, and collect it?' the men inquire. 'No,' he replied, 'for fear that while collecting the darnel you should at the same time root up the wheat with it. Leave both to grow together until the harvest, and at harvest-time I will direct the reapers, 'Collect the darnel first,*

and make it up into bundles to burn it, but bring all the wheat into my barn.'"

When he had dismissed the people and had returned to the house, his disciples came to him with the request, "Explain to us the parable of the darnel sown in the field."

"The sower of the good seed," he replied, "is the Son of Man; the field is the world; the good seed, these are the sons of the Kingdom; the darnel, the sons of the Evil one. The enemy who sows the darnel is the Devil; the harvest is the Close of the Age; the reapers are the angels. As then the darnel is collected together and burnt up with fire, so will it be at the Close of the Age. The Son of Man will commission his angels, and they will gather out of his Kingdom all causes of sin and all who violate his laws; and these they will throw into the fiery furnace. There will be the weeping aloud and the gnashing of teeth. Then will the righteous shine out like the sun in their Father's Kingdom. Listen, every one who has ears!"

They had all done their homework and knew that darnel was a weed which looked very much like wheat in the early stages. Melanie told them that again Jeremias had argued that the interpretation was evidently an addition; the Gospel of Thomas had the parable without the interpretation and the vocabulary of the interpretation was used to buttress his claim. "So what is the substitute interpretation?" she asked. "Jeremias says that it was originally to teach that this unpromising community, the twelve disciples and others, including many disreputable characters, was the beginning of the Kingdom. It also warned against seeking to become judgmental and trying to purify the group." They listened to this and commented that there wasn't so much difference between this and the interpretation in the text. With five more parables to consider, she pushed forward:

Another parable he put before them. "The Kingdom of Heaven," he said, "is like a mustard-seed, which a man takes and sows in his ground. It is the smallest of all seeds, and yet when full-grown it is larger than any herb and forms a tree, so that the birds come and build in its branches."

Another parable he spoke to them. "The Kingdom of Heaven," he said, "is like yeast which a woman takes and buries in a bushel of flour, for it to work there till the whole mass has risen."

They had no difficulty in seeing that there was again a reference to the insignificant beginnings and the disproportionate outcome. Some found it ironic that the fulfillment might be found in history with the growth of Christendom; some one quoted the saying of Alfred Loisy, the French biblical scholar who said: "Jesus preached the kingdom of God; but what came was the church." There was an inconclusive discussion about the question of Church and Kingdom: did Jesus anticipate anything like what exists today in his name?

> *All this Jesus spoke to the people in parables, and except in parables he spoke nothing to them, in fulfillment of the saying of the Prophet, "I will open my mouth in parables, I will utter things kept hidden since the creation of all things."*

Not surprisingly, Al wondered if Jesus had come to a time when he abandoned plain speech in favor of parables. "Was this to make it more difficult for his opponents to take issue with him?" Then there was a question about the quotation from Psalm 78 where the psalmist appears to be referring to his own utterance. It was pointed out that Psalm 78 contained nothing which could be called a parable and maybe this encouraged the thought that the ancient writer had in mind a future speaker.

Then two more:

> *"The Kingdom of Heaven is like treasure buried in the open country, which a man finds, but buries again, and, in his joy about it, goes and sells all he has and buys that piece of ground.*
> *Again the Kingdom of Heaven is like a jewel merchant who is in quest of choice pearls. He finds one most costly pearl; he goes away; and though it costs all he has, he buys it."*

Here at last, parables without any hint of interpretation and Melanie pointed out that although they were superficially similar, there were substantial differences. "In the first case, the discovery seems accidental while the other has a merchant who is always on the look out. In both cases the response is extreme: the treasure-finder acts in a morally dubious way but both he and the merchant liquidate all assets in order to achieve their heart's desire." Andrew asked if the interpretations gave rise to alternatives. "Maybe the treasure seeker and the merchant represent God seeking for his new community, the beginning of the Kingdom. Or, could it be that they represented people seeking for the Kingdom. I've heard sermons promoting both points of view."

"Let's take them separately," Melanie suggested. "There is a clear hint that the Kingdom is like treasure hidden and the response, from one who stumbles across buried treasure, is two fold. Total abandonment of possessions and even a hint of letting go of conventional morality!" Webster responded, "I have wondered about that. Is the concealment of the find quite honest?" They tossed that about for a bit and then Melanie gave her concept of the pearl merchant. "Now it is the Kingdom likened to the searcher who will sacrifice all to possess that one pearl. Is this God searching for his people and being willing to make any sacrifice to find them?"

She used her "power" to leave them to think about that and moved along:

> "Again the Kingdom of the Heavens is like a draw-net let down into the sea, which encloses fish of all sorts. When full, they haul it up on the beach, and sit down and collect the good fish in baskets, while the worthless they throw away. So will it be at the close of the age. The angels will go forth and separate the wicked from among the righteous, and will throw them into the fiery furnace. There will be the weeping aloud and the gnashing of teeth."

Al suggested that this was a bit like the Wheat and the Darnel. "The Kingdom contains all kinds of people and the sorting out is not to be done to the End." He couldn't help adding that if he were a fish, he would have some preference to be cast back into the sea!

They threw up their hands at the next bit; were the disciples to see themselves as a new kind of scribe?

> "Have you understood all this?" he asked. "Yes," they said. "Therefore," he said, "remember that every scribe well trained for the kingdom of Heaven is like a householder who brings out of his storehouse new things and old."

Stephen had something to share from his reading. "I don't know Greek but I have read that the verb 'ekballo' which is 'to bring out' in our text, more generally means 'to cast out'. Perhaps this is a radical suggestion of housecleaning with energy." They were tiring now and Melanie could scarcely get any attention for the last text:

> *Jesus concluded this series of parables and then departed. And he came into his own country and proceeded to teach in their synagogue, so that they were filled with astonishment and exclaimed, "Where did he obtain such wisdom, and these wondrous powers? Is not this the carpenter's son? Is not his mother called Mary? And are not his brothers, James, Joseph, Simon and Judah? And his sisters—are they not all living here among us? Where then did he get all this?" So they turned angrily away from him. But Jesus said to them, "There is no prophet left without honor except in his own country and among his own family." And he performed but few mighty deeds there because of their want of faith.*

Al reminded them of their discussions so long before, when they were studying Chapter 4 and came across the casual remark that Jesus moved house to Capernaum from Nazareth. "Do you remember how Webster steered us to Luke's gospel and the account of the violent expulsion from the synagogue at Nazareth? This sounds like another version of that same tradition." No one wished to argue. Someone was heard to murmur, "The night is far spent, the day is at hand," and allowing for some exaggeration, they could only agree that time was up!

Chapter 14

A NEW YEAR AND new challenges. Not least among them, the completion of their journey through Matthew's Gospel with, at last, the half way point in sight.

On a top shelf, Matty's Bible kept silent vigil. Melanie marveled again that, of its eleven hundred and fifty pages, the Gospel of Matthew occupied only thirty-four, about three per cent of the whole. And here they were, not yet half way and skimming the surface at that.

She had some time between Christmas and New Year with the office closed and the Tuesday night session cancelled by mutual consent. Melanie determined to read through the remainder of the Gospel.

It didn't take her long to see that Chapter 14 would be challenging with the feeding miracle and the walking on the water. Then the puzzling repetition of the feeding story in Chapter 15, the meaning of Peter's confession and the prediction of the Passion in Chapter 16, and the transfiguration in Chapter 17. Having read that far, she felt her resolve begin to weaken and she knew that reading to the end would be a challenge. Why was it so hard to read, she wondered. In her office, she could sit and read a fifty-page document of turgid legal exposition without trouble but this seemed to be in a different category altogether. It seemed to draw her in, to a place she would rather not go!

On Friday, she received a call from Andrew and she was somewhat surprised to hear from him. He wanted to meet with her and she wondered why.

They met at the coffee shop, now becoming familiar to Melanie as a place where she could learn about the reactions of various members of the group. After they had equipped themselves with lattes, Andrew went straight to the point. "It's been a good experience being in the group and your style is very different from Matty's." She waited for the "but" and it came. "But you have probably noticed how the discussion is carried along by three of four of us and I am wondering if there are people who find it a bit difficult to get a word in." She wondered whom he had in mind. "I take your point and it has been a concern to me, too," she said. "How did Matty handle it?" Andrew sipped his latte as he thought about this. "I guess," he said, "that she was willing to call on people for an opinion. And when I think about that," he continued, "I realize that not everyone found that quite comfortable!" They talked about this for a while and Melanie promised that she would try to encourage more general participation. Andrew wasn't finished. "There is also the question of the approach. Some of us feel that we are too analytical and that our various speculations lead us into frustration. Can't we just accept the text as it is? Many Christians find this very satisfying." Again she felt she needed to be a bit defensive. "You are paying the price of Matty's legacy to me to be your leader when my own ideas are so illformed." But she promised that she would take his concerns into account.

So when it was time to begin again, she took the opportunity to raise some of the matters that she had discussed with Andrew without naming their source. "I hope that you all feel free to join in the discussion at any time. Looking back on where we have been, it seems that several of us do more than our share of talking." Then she realized that she had not phrased that remark too tactfully and she tried again. "That's not to discourage anyone. I'm just thinking that we are all in this together." It still wasn't right and she had to go on and hope that no one was offended. "I have also been thinking," she continued, "that our line of approaching the text isn't the only one. There are many who simply take it at face value and some who might think that we are asking too many questions. I think that one can argue that Matthew's Gospel isn't a puzzle to be solved but rather a text which gives an opportunity for encounter." She stopped and the unusual silence told her that her attempt to exercise leadership was not satisfactory to everyone.

They were all glad to move on to the text:

> About that time Herod the Tetrarch heard of the fame of Jesus, and he said to his courtiers, "This is John the Baptist: he has come back to life—and that is why these miraculous Powers are working in him." For Herod had arrested John, and had put him in chains and imprisoned him, for the sake of Herodias, his brother Philip's wife, because John had persistently said to him, "It is not lawful for you to have her." And he would have liked to put him to death, but was afraid of the people, because they regarded John

> as a Prophet. But when Herod's birthday came, the daughter of Herodias danced before all the company, and so pleased Herod that with an oath he promised to give her whatever she asked. So she, instigated by her mother, said, "Give me here on a dish the head of John the Baptist." The king was deeply vexed, yet, because of his repeated oath and of the guests at his table, he ordered it to be given her, and he sent and beheaded John in the prison. The head was brought on a dish and given to the young girl, and she took it to her mother.

Al was ready to recall his memory of being in the Sydney Opera House when *Salome* was presented. He described the Oscar Wilde play on which the opera was based with the dramatic ending: Herod, utterly disgusted with Salome's licentious behaviour (*The Dance of the Seven Veils* and the kissing of the lips of the severed head) orders that she should be beheaded, too, and so the opera ends. Someone asked whether the name Salome was Wilde's invention and Al was able to forestall Webster, for once, by giving the information that the name occurs in Josephus, *The Antiquities of the Jews*. He even offered a discount on the thirteen volume set which had been on the shelves of his bookshop, as he said, "for too long." They agreed that the story was not one upon which they needed to linger! So again:

> Then John's disciples went and removed the body and buried it, and came and informed Jesus. Upon receiving these tidings, Jesus went away by boat to an uninhabited and secluded district; but the people heard of it and followed Him in crowds from the towns by land. So Jesus went out and saw an immense multitude, and felt compassion for them, and cured those of them who were afflicted.

Stephen remarked that this was a time of grief for Jesus and a time for solitude, and he recalled the death of his own father when he had felt the need for solitude and had been obliged to give classes the very next day. In retrospect, he thought that the distraction was probably good for him but he resented it at the time. Al remarked that while there might be "no rest for the wicked," there was often even less rest for those who were compassionate. "And the demands grew greater," remarked Melanie as she led them to the next section:

> *But when evening was come, the disciples came to him and said, "This is an uninhabited place, and the best of the day is now gone; send the people away to go into the villages and buy something to eat."*
>
> *"They need not go away," replied Jesus. "You yourselves must give them something to eat."*
>
> *"We have nothing here," they said, "but five loaves and a couple of fish."*
>
> *"Bring them here to me," he said, and he told all the people to sit down on the grass. Then he took the five loaves and the two fish, and after looking up to heaven and blessing them, he broke up the loaves and gave them to the disciples, and the disciples distributed them to the people. So all ate, and were fully satisfied. The broken portions that remained over they gathered up, filling twelve baskets. Those who had eaten were about five thousand men, without reckoning women and children.*

Melanie expressed some of her problems with this account. The people were not starving and there was an option: to go to neighboring villages. She also knew that accounts of the feeding miracles were highly popular among the early Christians. The Gospels contain six accounts, more or less similar. Webster again: "Do you recall the version given in John's Gospel where the feeding miracle is the basis for the long discourse on the bread which came down from heaven? He shocks the hostile crowd when he identifies that bread with himself and says, 'I am the living bread which came down from heaven and he that eats my flesh will never die.'" Al had never heard this before and was anxious to know chapter and verse. "This is a whole different world," was his verdict.

There was a discussion of the feeding miracle and its relation to the Eucharist. Stephen pointed out the four-fold action: taking bread, blessing it, breaking it and giving it to the disciples. "Exactly the same order as in the Last Supper."

Melanie was relieved that there was no inclination to look for an "explanation" of the event. She was aware that over the centuries there had been attempts to "explain away" such episodes. An attempt applied to this story had some appeal to her rational nature: that the sharing of the meager supply of food at the beginning encouraged others to share their own private rations with their neighbors. She was aware that Andrew, for one, wouldn't appreciate such speculations.

Martha had a final word. "Do you remember my theory that 'Matthew' might have been a woman? Well, here's another shred of evidence. Only 'Matthew' adds the little bit about women and children at the end of the story. The other Gospels leave it out. Think about it!" And think about it they did, but only for a moment before they went on:

> *Immediately afterwards he made the disciples go on board the boat and cross to the opposite shore, leaving him to dismiss the people. When he had done this, he climbed the hill to pray in solitude. Night came on, and he was there alone.*
>
> *Meanwhile the boat was far out on the Lake, buffeted and tossed by the waves, the wind being adverse. But towards daybreak he went to them, walking on the water. When the disciples saw him walking on the water, they were greatly alarmed. "It is a spirit," they exclaimed, and they cried out with terror. But instantly Jesus spoke to them, and said, "There is no danger; it is I; do not be afraid."*

If the feeding miracle was problematic, what about this? It wasn't clear that the disciples were in danger from the storm and if they were, a word from their master would have been enough. Stephen reminded them of the stilling of the storm episode in Chapter 8 and told of his discovery that the Greek word "epi" which is almost always translated as "on," could occasionally have the meaning "beside." "Could Jesus have simply been walking 'beside' the sea and, in the storm, his presence on the shore somehow alarmed them?" There was a good deal of opposition to this idea; that he "went to them" while remaining on the shore, seemed a contradiction and that they could carry on a conversation during a storm from ship to shore was also hard to believe. They went on to consider the next part of the story, with Webster pointing out that Mark's version of the episode ends without Peter's adventure:

> *"Master," answered Peter, "if it is you, bid me come to you upon the water."*
>
> *"Come," said Jesus. Then Peter climbed down from the boat and walked upon the water to go to him. But when he felt the wind he grew frightened, and, beginning to sink, he cried out, "Master, save me." Instantly Jesus stretched out his hand and caught hold of him, saying to him, "O little faith, why did you doubt?" So they climbed into the boat, and the wind lulled; and the men on board fell down before him and said, "You are indeed God's Son."*

Webster continued by pointing out the way that Mark's Gospel concludes the episode. He read out to them, "He got into the boat with them and the wind ceased. And they were utterly astounded for they did not understand about the loaves but their hearts were hardened." There was a discussion of this: did Matthew replace Mark's ending to put the disciples in a better light? In particular, did he wish to begin the special prominence that Peter would have in the rest of the Gospel with a story that shows him to be both brave and fearful?

This gave them plenty to talk about. Several had obviously used the "time off" to read ahead and Stephen, in particular, had a theory that perhaps there had been two documents which had been spliced together. "Listen," he said, "suddenly Peter becomes prominent from Chapter 15 to the end and secondly, there is the strange fact that, having told the feeding narrative in Chapter 14, it is repeated almost unchanged in the next chapter." Melanie felt that this was taking them into uncharted territory and she suggested that they should keep Stephen's theory in mind during the remaining weeks. She showed them, on the screen, the final part of the chapter:

> *When they had quite crossed over, they put ashore at Gennesaret; and the men of the place, recognizing him, sent word into all the country round. So they brought all the sick to him and they entreated him that they might but touch the tassel of his outer garment; and all who did so were restored to perfect health.*

They had little inclination to comment on this and so they went away, having had a busy evening. Melanie reflected on her failure to bring more participants into the conversation and wondered if Andrew had gone away disappointed. She wished that he had been able to set the pace by being more active himself but realized that she couldn't force change on them. They were, after all, grown ups!

Chapter 15

MELANIE WAS STILL UNHAPPY the next day about some aspects of the previous night's session and she phoned Andrew, discovering, to her surprise, that he was comfortable with what had happened. He rather took the words from her mouth with his comment, "You opened the door. Now it's up to us to enter!" Then she suggested that he might wish to take leadership for a session but he declined. "I will come next time better prepared. It had dawned on me that those who say the most are the ones who are doing the most reading and thinking about the text." Drawing some reassurance from this, she decided to set aside her misgivings and proceed as before.

Sure enough on the following Tuesday, she had scarcely put up the first section, when Andrew wanted to speak. "I appreciate that Melanie is trying to encourage a wider participation from among us and I should apologize that I haven't been more active. But I have been doing some reading about the Pharisees this week and have some things to say about this text." The body language of the group and their evident attention encouraged him to continue: "I came across a book by Jacob Neusner on the Pharisees. Neusner is a prolific writer on Judaism and he claims that the Pharisees were an insignificant group until the destruction of the Second Temple in 70 A.D. From this, he deduces that the prominent role they play in the Gospels reflects a later period when they were the principal opponents of the young Christian Church. Therefore, he argues, the disputes with the Pharisees can't be original but represent a construction of the writer of the Gospel." He paused and Melanie was concerned that they were going to get a full lecture on this topic. However, Al chimed in with the comment that they had encountered this question before and that they had struggled with the idea that Matthew could get away with such interpolations. "I agree," said Andrew. "I am convinced that even if the Pharisees were few in number, they represented something profoundly at odds with what Jesus was proclaiming. It has already been mentioned that their insistence on ritual purity would exclude all but well-to-do people who had the resources to follow the prescription about hand washing, for example."

While he had been speaking, Melanie displayed the text:

> *Then there came to Jesus a party of Pharisees and Scribes from Jerusalem, who inquired, "Why do your disciples transgress the tradition of the Elders by not washing their hands before meals?"*
>
> *"Why do you, too," he retorted, "transgress God's commands for the sake of your tradition? For God said, 'Honour thy father and thy mother'; and 'Let him who reviles father or mother be certainly put to death'; but you—this is what you say: 'If a man says to his father or mother, That is consecrated, whatever it is, which otherwise you should have received from me— he shall be absolved from honoring his father'; and so you have abrogated God's Word for the sake of your tradition. Hypocrites! Well did Isaiah prophesy of you, 'This is a people who honor Me with their lips, while their heart is far away from Me; but it is in vain they worship Me, while they lay down precepts which are mere human rules.'"*

Andrew had some things to say also about the "Corban" tradition that allowed someone to dedicate property to God and thereby exclude it from other uses. It was not clear, he said, if the abuse indicated by the text, was a common practice (Neusner didn't think so). Perhaps some scandalous example was known to Jesus and his hearers.

As if this wasn't enough, he had something to say about the next section. Melanie hoped that she wouldn't lose control of the evening!

> *Then, when he had called the people to him, Jesus said, "Hear and understand. It is not what goes into a man's mouth that defiles him; but it is what comes out of his mouth—that defiles a man."*
>
> *Then his disciples came and said to him, "Do you know that the Pharisees were greatly shocked when they heard those words?"*
>
> *"Every plant," he replied, "which my Heavenly Father has not planted will be rooted up. Leave them alone. They are blind guides of the blind; and if a blind man leads a blind man, both will fall into some pit."*
>
> *"Explain to us this figurative language," said Peter.*

> "Are even you," he answered, "still without intelligence? Do you not understand that whatever enters the mouth passes into the stomach and is afterwards ejected from the body? But the things that come out of the mouth proceed from the heart, and it is these that defile the man. For out of the heart proceed wicked thoughts, murder, adultery, fornication, theft, perjury, and impiety of speech. These are the things which defile the man; but eating with unwashed hands does not defile."

Anticipating a question, Andrew explained that impurity was thought to be transmissible by touch so that anyone who had touched an unclean object or person automatically became unclean and so did you if they touched you. Then eating without washing of the hands brought the greatest peril of all: consuming unclean food. The disciples' incomprehension is now centered on Peter, for the discussion has taken an unexpected turn. True defilement is from within, not from some impure food. Webster, who had listened attentively to all of this, interrupted with the comment that in Mark's Gospel, after the phrase ". . . and is afterwards ejected from the body," there is the comment, "In saying this, Jesus declares all foods clean." He went on to say, "Matthew omits this and scholarly opinion is rather united in the belief that it is an interpolation from a later date. The issue isn't about pure and impure foods but about the necessity of hand washing and the true origin of impurity." The interruption was timely as it seemed to put Andrew off his path and he relapsed into silence. Was it time to move on? Melanie thought so and displayed the next section, inviting Martha to comment:

> Leaving that place, Jesus withdrew into the vicinity of Tyre and Sidon. Here a Canaanitish woman of the district came out and persistently cried out, "Sir, Son of David, pity me; my daughter is cruelly harassed by a demon." But he answered her not a word. Then the disciples interposed, and begged him, saying, "Send her away because she keeps crying behind us."
>
> "I have only been sent to the lost sheep of the house of Israel," he replied.
>
> Then she came and threw herself at his feet and entreated him. "O Sir, help me," she said.
>
> "It is not right," he said, "to take the children's bread and throw it to the dogs."

> "Be it so, Sir," she said, "for even the dogs eat the scraps which fall from their masters' tables."
>
> "O woman," replied Jesus, "great is your faith: be it done to you, as you desire." And from that moment her daughter was restored to health.

Martha reminded them that they had worked on this passage with Matty when they did "Women in the Bible". She commented that it had become widely believed that Jesus himself entered a new understanding of his ministry through this encounter. The national identity of the woman put her among the traditional enemies of Israel and her place of residence in the old territory of the Philistines was another count against her. "The very fact that she was a woman would normally exclude her from contact with a man outside her family. It wasn't surprising that Jesus is taken aback, ('he answered her not a word'), and that the disciples wanted nothing to do with her."

The resistance which Jesus shows, on the grounds that he had a limited mandate to proclaim the Kingdom only to his own people, is overcome. The response, more correctly translated, ". . . even the little puppies eat the scraps . . ." is a witty piece of repartee. And she is praised for her faith, contrasting her with Peter who, in the previous chapter, is described as one of little faith.

Stephen wanted to know what Jesus was doing in the region. "He'd had little success in finding solitude. Maybe he decided to take a day at the beach." He wondered if, from that point on, Jesus showed more openness to Gentiles. Webster reminded him that the order in which events appeared in a Gospel couldn't be considered as chronological since each Gospel presented different orders. "We can't know if this event took place early or late." He also reminded them of their discussion when they encountered the healing of the centurion's servant in Chapter 8 with the similar commendation of "great faith."

> *Again, moving thence, Jesus went along by the Lake of Galilee; and ascending the hill, he sat down there. Soon great crowds came to him, bringing with them those who were crippled in feet or hands, blind or dumb, and many besides, and they hastened to lay them at his feet. And he cured them, so that the people were amazed to see the dumb speaking, the maimed with their hands perfect, the lame walking, and the blind seeing; and they gave the glory to the God of Israel.*

As they considered this with an eye on the similar narrative in the previous chapter, they noticed that the setting was rather different, seemingly not remote, certainly close enough to villages that the lame could be carried to where Jesus was. Also Chapter 14 suggests that the crowd had been gathered only for a single day whereas in the following, they were three days away from home. Stephen, in particular, was eager to follow up on his theory that he had advanced the previous week. "It has the same structure and the difference in details suggests that it had been told over and over again."

Then, on to the second feeding story:

> But Jesus called his disciples to him and said, "My heart yearns over this mass of people, for it is now the third day that they have been with me and they have nothing to eat. I am unwilling to send them away hungry, lest they should faint on the road."
>
> "Where can we," asked the disciples, "get bread enough in this remote place to satisfy so vast a multitude?"
>
> "How many loaves have you?" Jesus asked. "Seven," they said, "and a few small fish."
>
> So he bade all the people sit down on the ground, and he took the seven loaves and the fish, and after giving thanks he broke them up and then distributed them to the disciples, and they to the people. And they all ate and were satisfied. The broken portions that remained over they took up—seven full hampers. Those who ate were four thousand men, without reckoning women and children.
>
> He then dismissed the people, went on board the boat, and came into the district of Magadan.

He found it very hard to believe that anyone who was skilful enough to compose a "gospel" would be so clumsy as to repeat the same story. There was some discussion about this with a reminder that traditionally it had been believed that these were separate events. "Even if they had been," insisted Stephen, "why record them both?" As usual, such questions were more easily asked than answered and they all seemed content to call it a day.

Chapter 16

Stephen sent her an email on Wednesday morning, claiming to have more evidence for his "two document" hypothesis. Melanie hoped that he wasn't becoming obsessed with this idea but she promised to give him time to explain his "discovery" to the group. She couldn't get too excited about his idea and worried that he might get off on a tangent.

However, when they met and she showed the first section, he was ready to go:

> Here the Pharisees and Sadducees came to him; and, to make trial of him, they asked him to show them a sign in the sky. He replied, "In the evening you say, 'It will be fine weather, for the sky is red,' and in the morning, 'It will be rough weather to-day, for the sky is red and murky.' You learn how to distinguish the aspect of the heavens, but the signs of the times you cannot. A wicked and faithless generation are eager for a sign; but none shall be given to them except the sign of Jonah." And he left them and went away.

He asked to say something about the Sadducees and explained that they were another sect among the Jewish people, very different from the Pharisees. They were supporters of the priesthood and the Temple. As well, they restricted themselves to the Torah, the five books of Moses and allowed no subsequent authority. He passed over this rather quickly so that he could reveal what he had discovered: that the second part of Matthew's Gospel in which he had pointed out the repetition of the feeding miracle and the increased role of Peter, also had the Sadducees suddenly being mentioned six times whereas in the first part they had only been mentioned once, and that in relation to John the Baptist. Nobody seemed much impressed and Al commented that he was aware that there were many theories about the composition of the Gospel and suggested that they should keep away from them all as distractions from reading the text. Stephen was rather crestfallen when no one came to his defense and Melanie hoped that the matter wouldn't come up again. Al continued with a question, "What kind of 'sign' would have satisfied them? Maybe a comet or an eclipse?" Webster commented that most translations gave the text as "a sign from heaven" and suggested that, had they stayed around for a while, they would have seen plenty of "signs." Then there was discussion about the "sign of Jonah" which had first been encountered in Chapter 12. Melanie was ready for Stephen to see this request for a sign for what it was: a repetition of the episode of that previous chapter, further evidence for his "theory" but Stephen kept silent, perhaps biding his time. And since that was a good time to move on, she did:

> *When the disciples arrived at the other side of the Lake, they found that they had forgotten to bring any bread; and when Jesus said to them, "See to it: beware of the yeast of the Pharisees and Sadducees," they reasoned among themselves, saying, "It is because we have not brought any bread."*
>
> *Jesus perceived this and said, "Why are you reasoning among yourselves, you men of little faith, because you have no bread? Do you not yet understand, nor even remember the five thousand and the five loaves, and how many basketfuls you carried away, nor the four thousand and the seven loaves, and how many hampers you carried away? How is it you do not understand that it was not about bread that I spoke to you? But beware of the yeast of the Pharisees and Sadducees."*
>
> *Then they perceived that he had not warned them against bread-yeast, but against the teaching of the Pharisees and Sadducees.*

Melanie admitted that she found this rather confusing as, evidently, the disciples did. Al wondered why Jesus addressed them again as "men of little faith" when it seemed that they were simply confused. "Once again, it seems that something was going on and we can't know what it was. Maybe it was clearer in the original." There was no evidence that anyone had new ideas about this. Melanie felt, as she often did, that they hadn't done justice to this section but she moved along, nevertheless:

> *When he arrived in the neighbourhood of Caesarea Philippi, Jesus questioned his disciples. "Who do people say that the Son of Man is?" he asked. "Some say John the Baptist," they replied; "others Elijah; others Jeremiah or one of the Prophets."*

> "But you, who do you say that I am?" he asked again. "You," replied Simon Peter, "are the Christ, the Son of the ever-living God."
>
> "Blessed are you, Simon bar-Jonah," said Jesus, "for mere human nature has not revealed this to you, but my Father in Heaven. And I declare to you that you are Peter, and that upon this Rock I will build my church, and the might of Hades shall not triumph over it. I will give you the keys of the Kingdom of Heaven; and whatever you bind on earth shall remain bound in heaven, and whatever you loose on earth shall remain loosed in heaven."

They had all done their homework about this. The old problem of this curious way of referring to himself as "Son of Man" was briefly revisited with Stephen needing to comment that "Son of Man" is used much more frequently in the second half of Matthew than in the first. But the notion of "binding and loosing" attracted the main discussion. Webster had read that "binding" and "loosing" were technical terms applied to situations in which the Law was to be applied or not: so, for example, the Law says "Thou shalt not steal," and the commentators had discussed the question of when a found object should be returned to its owner. He quoted that vast collection of legal opinion, the Talmud, "If a fledgling bird is found within fifty cubits of a dovecote, it belongs to the owner of the dovecote. If it is found outside the limits of fifty cubits, it belongs to the person who finds it"

"This helped me understand the ideas of 'binding' and 'loosing'," he remarked. "In one case the law applies and in the other it doesn't." Andrew looked puzzled. "Does this mean that Peter was given authority to act as a kind of a judge?" Martha, drawing on her Catholic education, recalled the teaching of her church that, indeed, Peter and his successor bishops of Rome had been given the power to establish doctrine in the church and that their decisions on such matters were ratified in heaven.

They all knew that Peter, in Greek, "petros," was the word for "rock" and that the change of name from "Simon" to "Peter" indicated a transition at the deepest level. Andrew recalled, "There is a story of Jacob in the Jewish scriptures, whose name meant 'heel grabber'. He wrestles with God and becomes 'Israel', the 'god wrestler'". Stephen wanted to look ahead and he remarked that it seemed that whenever Peter is commended, it almost always follows that he is rebuked: they would notice how soon he is addressed as "Satan". Before Melanie would move along to this episode, however, she wanted to discuss the use of the word "church" in the promise to Peter. "Was Jesus looking into the future to the founding of a church in the sense that we know it? Or did he simply refer to a community forming around Peter and the other disciples?"

She mentioned that she had found, among the documents left to her by Aunt Matty, a copy of a book by Oscar Cullmann, entitled "Peter". She mentioned it to point out that Cullmann devoted eighty three pages of detailed discussion of these verses as a reminder of the vast sea of scholarship in which they were placing a toe! They were suitably impressed. "Onwards," was the cry!

> *Then he urged his disciples to tell no one that he was the Christ. From this time Jesus began to explain to his disciples that he must go to Jerusalem, and suffer much cruelty from the elders and the High Priests and the scribes, and be put to death, and on the third day be raised to life again. Then Peter took him aside and began taking him to task. "Master," he said, "God forbid; this will not be your lot." But he turned and said to Peter, "Get behind me, Satan; you are a hindrance to me, because your thoughts are not God's thoughts, but men's."*

This is the first prediction of the Passion and Peter was having none of it. Stephen remarked that Peter's rise to prominence seemed always to put him in an ambiguous light. He reminded them of his brave attempt to "walk on water" and the crushing rebuke, "you of little faith." And if this were not enough, having now been given extraordinary power, the keys of the Kingdom, the right to bind and release, he is called "Satan." "It seems as though Matthew wished to affirm Peter's role as leader but always with a reminder of the flawed nature of that leadership."

As for the prediction which Jesus gave of his death, Andrew wondered if he had come by it from putting together the verses from Isaiah about the Suffering Servant, the text in the book of the prophet Hosea, *After two days, he will revive us; on the third day he will restore us, that we may live in his presence,* and the sign of Jonah. "It is possible that he might conclude that his messianic destiny would be along a path of suffering, death and resurrection." Al wondered if that insight might have included anticipation of crucifixion. "The next verse suggests that he had something like that in mind." Melanie took that as an invitation to display the remainder of the chapter:

Then Jesus said to his disciples, "If any one desires to follow me, let him renounce self and take up his cross and so be my follower. For whoever desires to save his life shall lose it, and whoever loses his life for my sake shall find it. Why, what benefit will it be to a man if he gains the whole world but forfeits his life? Or what shall a man give to buy back his life?

For the Son of Man is soon to come in the glory of the Father with His angels, and then will he requite every man according to his actions. I solemnly tell you that some of those who are standing here will certainly not taste death till they have seen the Son of Man coming in his kingdom."

Webster wondered what the disciples thought when "taking up the cross" was first mentioned. It was a horrifying image in the ancient world; "going to the gallows" might have carried something like it to our parents' generation but it is difficult, he claimed, to overstate the horror and humiliation associated with crucifixion in the Roman world. There was some discussion and the consensus which was reached included the probability that the section on display was probably spoken at a later time.

And speaking of later time, they agreed that they had reached it and so they dispersed, again feeling benefit but frustration.

Chapter 17

That week, Melanie was again preoccupied with her other life and didn't spend much time preparing for Matthew 17. But, after a brief perusal, she could see that the Transfiguration narrative would be challenging. It was almost irresistible to ask, "What happened?" rather than, "What does this mean?" She wondered if they would become bogged down in speculations about the nature of the event.

So on Tuesday she expressed some of these concerns and received a lukewarm reception. "We really do need to spend a bit of time trying to figure out what happened," said Al. He asked for the text to be shown:

> *Six days later, Jesus took Peter and the brothers James and John, and brought them up a high mountain to a solitary place. There in their presence his form underwent a change; his face shone like the sun, and his raiment became as white as the light. And suddenly Moses and Elijah appeared to them conversing with him. Then Peter said to Jesus, "Master, we are thankful to you that we are here. If you approve, I will put up three tents here, one for you, one for Moses, and one for Elijah." He was still speaking when a luminous cloud spread over them; and a voice was heard from within the cloud, which said, "This is My Son dearly beloved, in whom is My delight. Listen to Him." On hearing this voice, the disciples fell on their faces and were filled with terror. But Jesus came and touched them, and said, "Rouse yourselves and have no fear." So they looked up, and saw no one but Jesus.*

He had questions. "What is this, 'six days later' business? Luke says 'eight days' and it is a new style of writing for Matthew to try to connect episodes this way. And why choose three disciples? Not exactly a good way to build community." Al was evidently in a combative mood and no one had any answers to his questions. But Stephen said, "Maybe there had been some original mystical experience which had been part of the 'Jesus memory'. If so, then the story which we read is a development from some unknown source. Could it be that the 'six days' were related to the 'six days of creation'? The beginning of a new creation. Or 'six days' in which work was permitted with the 'after six days' indicating the ultimate Sabbath of the Kingdom." Al was impressed. "That's very plausible but what about the choice of Peter, James and John?" he responded. Stephen was on a roll. He proposed that when Matthew was writing, it was necessary to emphasize the leadership of the three. "After all, they are traditionally authors of six books of the New Testament."

The evening was taking a different direction from that which Melanie had envisioned and there was some discussion on the nature of mystical experience. No one seemed to know if such experiences could be truly shared but some felt that religious rituals could give some shared experiences of the Divine. "After all, for some people, part of the motivation to gather, Sunday by Sunday, might be some expectation of such events," Andrew proposed There was a confused discussion of church going and its possible benefits. "Surely," said Melanie, "most people who go to church aren't expecting a 'religious experience'; as a truant from Sunday worship for these many years, I can only guess what motivates people to get up on a Sunday morning and sit in an uncomfortable pew."

"But what about the meaning of this text?" she continued. "I have come across the belief that Jesus is showing his true nature." Webster had something to contribute: "Two points," he said. "Firstly, I am puzzled that John's Gospel, which is so eager to present Jesus as the only begotten Son of God, doesn't mention this episode. And secondly, I have wondered if the prediction in Chapter 16, remember it, ' . . . some standing here will not taste of death before they see the Son of Man coming in his Kingdom,' could find its fulfillment here. The Transfiguration as a kind of a glimpse into the future." They were all impressed by this but there was nothing new offered so they went on:

> As they were descending the mountain, Jesus instructed them: "Tell no one," he said, "of the sight you have seen till the Son of Man has risen from among the dead."

Here, they agreed, was another one of those mysterious sayings. Could the three who had gone up the mountain not even share their experience with the other disciples? Al tried to imagine a conversation, "Welcome back, fellows. What have you been doing?"

"Sorry. Can't tell you. We were up the mountain."

"Any new commandments?"

"Please don't ask."

It was agreed that it would be a tense time, especially when the nine remaining disciples were forced to confront what they had been doing, or rather trying to do. But before that reunion, was a question to be considered:

> "Why then," asked the disciples, "do the scribes say that Elijah must first come?"
>
> "Elijah was indeed to come," he replied, "and would reform everything. But I tell you that he has already come, and they did not recognize him, but dealt with him as they chose. And before long the Son of Man will be treated by them in a similar way." Then it dawned upon the disciples that it was John the Baptist about whom he had spoken to them.

The group recalled a previous discussion about the identity of John the Baptist and didn't feel much inclination to revisit it. So, onwards:

> When they had returned to the people, there came to him a man who fell on his knees before Him and besought him "Sir," he said, "have pity on my son, for he is an epileptic and is very ill. Often he falls into the fire and often into the water. I have brought him to your disciples, and they have not been able to cure him."
>
> "O unbelieving and perverse generation!" replied Jesus; "how long shall I be with you? how long shall I endure you? Bring him to me."
>
> Then Jesus reprimanded the demon, and it came out and left him; and the boy was cured from that moment.

Webster was impressed that it seemed that this chapter was constructed to give a continuous narrative with triumphant events up the mountain and failure down below. But his main observation was from the comparison with the same episode as Mark's Gospel relates it. "It is difficult for me to accept the belief that Matthew knew Mark's version as he wrote. If he did, there is the strange omission of the lengthy discussion with the father of the afflicted boy and in particular, the challenge which Jesus gives: 'All things are possible to him who believes,' with the father's response: 'I believe; help my unbelief.' How would Matthew omit such a memorable exchange?" As usual, it was easier to ask such questions than to answer them. Al wanted to complain again about the rough treatment that the nine disciples seemed to get. "Not only are they left behind and kept in the dark about the events on the mountain but now rebuked in no uncertain terms. What was going on to make Jesus so cranky?"

It was time to continue:

> *Then the disciples came to Jesus privately and asked him, "Why could not we expel the demon?"*
> *"Because your faith is so small," he replied; "yet I solemnly declare to you that if you have faith like a mustard-seed, you shall say to this mountain, 'Remove from this place to that,' and it will remove; and nothing shall be impossible to you. But an evil spirit of this kind is only driven out by prayer and fasting."*

They agreed that there was a paradoxical explanation given: their small faith prevented them casting out the demon, yet faith even as small as a mustard seed would suffice to allow incredible miracles and unlimited powers. Stephen wondered if the "prayer and fasting" reference was added later. "It doesn't seem to fit and Jesus didn't take time out for prayer and fasting but apparently exorcised the demon without delay. In any case, this seems to be the only time when Jesus tells his disciples to fast."

Melanie felt that they were making little progress so she moved them along:

> *As they were travelling about in Galilee, Jesus said to them, "The Son of Man is about to be betrayed into the hands of men; they will put him to death, but on the third day he will be raised to life again." And they were exceedingly distressed.*

This seemed to be a repetition of the prediction of Chapter 16 and this time, the disciples' response is one of grief rather than argument.

It had been a long evening and Melanie was glad to set before them the last section of the chapter:

> *After Jesus and his disciples arrived at Capernaum, the collectors of the head tax came to Peter and asked, "Does not your Teacher pay the half-shekel?"*
> *"Yes," he replied, and then went into the house. But before he spoke a word Jesus said, "What think you, Simon? From whom do*

this world's kings receive customs or the head tax? from their own children, or from others?"

"From others," he replied.

"Then the children go free," said Jesus. "However, lest we cause them to sin, go and throw a hook into the Lake, and take the first fish that comes up. When you open its mouth, you will find a shekel in it bring that coin and give it to them for yourself and me."

Webster pointed out that none of the other Gospels had this episode and Stephen thought that it was like a folk tale. "Or a fisherman's tall story," suggested Al.

They agreed that it was an awkward story, and Webster reminded them that there were other "gospels," not included in the Bible, which were keen on this kind of thing. It was too late to explore this but Webster offered to give details to anyone who wanted them. The response was modest and it was time to go.

Chapter 18

Looking back to Tuesday evening, Melanie realized that her lack of preparation had effected the quality of the discussion. She was determined that she would find time, come what may, to prevent this from happening again. In line with her good intention, she read Chapter 18 on Friday evening and tried to anticipate where the discussion might lead. That night, no doubt influenced by her reading, she dreamed of her childhood and Aunt Matty. She was a sad five-year-old again, revisiting the pain of her mother's death and her father's increasing withdrawal from life. In her dream, she and Matty were in a church, looking at the stained glass. There was Jesus and the children, in all its sentimental Victorian splendor, with Jesus represented as blonde haired and blue eyed. Aunt Matty was telling her that the real Jesus would look quite different and as she stood there, the children faded and became the members of the Tuesday group, angry with her for disturbing them. She was running from the church when she awoke, sweaty and frightened. It was some time before she slept and she was somewhat disturbed by the memory of those angry faces. She wondered if the references to forgiveness in the text had been reflected in her dream and if the true anger was hers!

With such thoughts in mind, she arrived at the Tuesday session, somewhat troubled. However, the discussion was brisk and any thoughts of anger seem to drift away.

> *Just then the disciples came to Jesus and asked, "Who ranks higher than others in the Kingdom of Heaven?" So he called a young child to him, and, bidding him stand in the midst of them, said, "In solemn truth I tell you that unless you turn and become like little children, you will in no case be admitted into the Kingdom of Heaven. Whoever therefore shall humble himself as this young child, is superior to others in the Kingdom of Heaven. And whoever for my sake receives one young child such as this, receives me. But whoever shall occasion the fall of one of these*

little ones who believe in me, it would be better for him to have a millstone hung round his neck and to be drowned in the depths of the sea."

Andrew wondered why children were chosen as models. "As a father, I can love my children and I do, but they are never very humble in my experience." Webster had some things to say about the lowly status of children in the ancient world. "Even though having a son was the means by which one might continue to live on after death, yet children were powerless until they came of age." There was discussion about this and Stephen suggested that the word "humble" might refer to status rather than behavior. "As a child was totally dependent on parents, so the disciple should strive to become totally dependent on God." Andrew, who had some knowledge of Greek, pointed out that the reference to "children" changes to subsequent references in the text to "little ones"; two different words in Greek. "Is it possible that the reference to 'the little ones who believe in me' might be a new theme? Not only a new word but there is the additional aspect of 'believing in me' " The discussion was quite spirited, some agreeing with Andrew but others thinking that the reference, "<u>these</u> little ones" was decisive. But Andrew could remind them of the last verse of Chapter 10:

And whoever gives one of these little ones even a cup of cold water to drink because he is a disciple, I solemnly tell you that he will not lose his reward.

And there the discussion rested. They were directed by the PowerPoint display to consider:

"Alas for the world because of causes of falling! They are inevitable, but alas for each man through whom they come! If your hand or your foot is causing you to fall into sin, cut it off and away with it. It is better for you to enter into life crippled in hand or foot than to remain in possession of two sound hands or feet but be thrown into eternal fire.

And if your eye is causing you to fall into sin, tear it out and away with it; it is better for you to enter into life with only one eye, than to remain in possession of two eyes but be thrown into the Gehenna of fire."

Al remarked that the "falling" was a connection with the "fall of these little ones who believe in me" and wondered why the causes were "inevitable." He avoided getting the previous discussion going again by framing his question carefully: "Whether 'little ones' are children or disciples, does it mean that, in the nature of things, there will be 'causes of falling'? And if so, how should those through whom they come be so blameworthy?" No one wanted to try to answer and the conversation moved on to the passage about self-mutilation. Webster could remind them that they had encountered this same passage in Chapter 5 and had rather avoided discussing it. He thought that, in both cases, Jesus was deliberately exaggerating to make sure that the hearers took seriously what he was saying, a common rhetorical device. They wished again to talk about the threat of eternal fire and Gehenna. They recalled the earlier suggestion that the threat was related to the fires of the valley of Hinnon, which burned endlessly, refueled daily by the refuse of Jerusalem (and the bodies of criminals). Out of this concrete reality, perhaps the most ghastly destiny that they could envision, had emerged the doctrines of hellfire and everlasting damnation. Martha recalled her Catholic upbringing and the manner in which children of her time had been terrified by thoughts of Hell. She thought it ironic that she, as a child, had found this a "cause for falling," in her case into unbelief. She wanted to recall the more positive teaching she had received, however, from the next verse, which Melanie obligingly displayed:

> "Beware of ever despising one of these little ones, for I tell you that in Heaven their angels have continual access to my Father who is in Heaven."

She confessed that she still found comfort in the idea of the "guardian angel" and wondered what the "continual access" meant; asking God to intervene, maybe, in which case the intervention was often not very effective. The discussion drifted to mention of Curtis Sliwa and his somewhat controversial "Guardian Angels" with their peacekeeping activities in New York City and elsewhere. Such digressions challenged Melanie to keep moving on and so she did:

> "What do you think? Suppose a man gets a hundred sheep and one of them strays away, will he not leave the ninety-nine on the hills and go and look for the one that is straying. And if he succeeds in finding it, in solemn truth I tell you that he rejoices over it more than he does over the ninety-nine that have not gone astray.

> *Just so it is not the will of your Father in Heaven that one of these little ones should be lost."*

Al wondered if Matthew had a file marked "little ones" and gathered the material into one place. He couldn't see much continuity. But he could see this as a startling representation of a reckless love. "What happens to the other sheep?" he asked. "Are they left defenseless?" There were proposals that perhaps a flock of a hundred would have more than one shepherd or that the ninety-nine could be left safely in an enclosure. Webster reminded them of John's Gospel chapter 10 in which Jesus speaks of himself as the Good Shepherd and the sheep safely kept in a gated sheepfold.

Melanie had some things to say before she put up the next section. "If you have been reading any of the commentaries, you will know the general opinion that this next section comes from the early church. It envisions conflict resolution in a structured community." They looked at:

> *"If your brother acts wrongly towards you, go and point out his fault to him when only you and he are there. If he listens to you, you have gained your brother. But if he will not listen to you, go again, and ask one or two to go with you, that every word spoken may be attested by two or three witnesses. If he refuses to hear them, appeal to the Church; and if he refuses to hear even the Church, regard him just as you regard a Gentile or a tax-gatherer. I solemnly tell you that whatever you as a Church bind on earth will in Heaven be held as bound, and whatever you loose on earth will in Heaven be held to be loosed. I also solemnly tell you that if two of you here on earth agree together concerning anything whatever that you shall ask, it will be given to them from my Father who is in Heaven. For where there are two or three assembled in my name, there am I in the midst of them."*

Al was eager to tackle this and began by questioning its practicality. "Suppose," he said, "that I am in a dispute with you. Let's be specific; Melanie owes me fifty dollars and refuses to pay because she says she has already paid it. Now what? The whole text suggests that one party is clearly in the wrong and that everyone acknowledges it. Then we go through the three-step process that might lead to excommunication. But do you see how it could easily be turned around. I might initiate the process against Melanie but she might equally initiate it against me."

Melanie agreed, on the basis of her legal training, that Al had given a good argument. "But suppose," she said, "that it is addressed to the leaders of the community, giving them the right to initiate the process against an erring member. Then it makes some kind of sense, although open to abuse. Look at the next verses which indicate a decision of 'the church,' ratified in Heaven."

She went on to express her uncertainty about the two verses which follow, one giving reassurance about prayer and the other about the presence of Jesus when two or three are gathered. "It is as though Matthew, having mentioned the need for two or three witnesses, is then distracted towards other situations where 'two or three' have potency." Stephen remarked that when they encountered the teaching on prayer in the Sermon on the Mount, it seemed that asking was enough. "Now you must find someone who agrees with you in your request." The final comment came from Webster who suggested that the promise, "there am I in the midst of them," gave strong evidence for this being early church material. "It wouldn't make much sense when Jesus was standing right there."

Feeling that they had tidied up that particular section, Melanie felt less guilty than usual about pushing ahead:

> At this point Peter came to him with the question, "Master, how often shall my brother act wrongly towards me and I forgive him? seven times?"
>
> "I do not say seven times," answered Jesus, "but seventy times seven."
>
> "For this reason the Kingdom of Heaven may be compared to a king who determined to have a settlement of accounts with his servants. But as soon as he began the settlement, one was brought before him who owed ten thousand talents, and was unable to pay. So his master ordered that he and his wife and children and everything that he had should be sold, and payment be made. The servant therefore falling down, prostrated himself at his feet and entreated him. 'Only give me time,' he said, 'and I will pay you the whole.' Whereupon his master, touched with compassion, set him free and forgave him the debt. But no sooner had that servant gone out, than he met with one of his fellow servants who owed him a hundred pence; and seizing him by the throat and nearly stran-

gling him he exclaimed, 'Pay me all you owe.' His fellow servant therefore fell at his feet and entreated him, 'Only give me time,' he said, 'and I will pay you.' He would not, however, but went and threw him into prison until he should pay what was due. His fellow servants, therefore, seeing what had happened, were exceedingly angry; and they came and told their master without reserve all that had happened. At once his master called him and said, 'Wicked servant, I forgave you all that debt, because you entreated me: ought not you also to have had pity on your fellow servant, just as I had pity on you?' So his master, greatly incensed, handed him over to the jailers until he should pay all he owed him.

In the same way my Heavenly Father will deal with you, if you do not all of you forgive one another from your hearts."

They had all read this and Al remarked on its incongruity in view of the previous section. "We have been given rules which are very legalistic and suddenly the notion of forgiveness is introduced. And not only introduced, but emphasized about as strongly as one could imagine. Why such a contrast?" The discussion was inconclusive with most supporting Melanie's distinction, the difference between a private dispute and one in which the leadership of the church was being challenged.

As for the parable, the usual exaggeration was identified. Someone had found a reference to the province of Judaea whose total tax burden was six hundred talents. The idea of a master loaning anyone, let alone a slave, ten thousand talents and that the slave, seeking time, would promise to pay off the debt, would strike the hearers as absurd. Stephen reminded them of the Sermon on the Mount and the remark after the giving of the Lord's Prayer: "If you do not forgive, you will not be forgiven." He was struck by this way of teaching the same thing and wondered why Christians didn't take it more seriously. "I guess that justification by faith sounds a bit more manageable," he concluded. And on that note, they separated in a thoughtful frame of mind.

Chapter 19

Later that week, she met George Anderson in the hallway of their office. Not for the first time, he reminded her of the fateful moment when he had discharged his duty by delivering Aunt Matty's parcel and its unwelcome letter. He gently teased her about the task she had undertaken, "Matty's Legacy" as he termed it.

Melanie took the opportunity to draw on his experience as the chancellor of the local Roman Catholic Diocese. "Next Tuesday, we tackle Matthew 19 with the famous passage about divorce. Sometime you must tell me about how it works in your church." Later that same day, he delivered a booklet on that subject and remarked that he wasn't a theologian but he was bothered by some aspects of his duties on the question of annulment. "You probably know that the Roman Church doesn't permit remarriage after divorce and so we have the process of annulment by which the first marriage is shown to be in some way defective and therefore not really a marriage at all." Melanie had been aware of this idea. "It must be hard on children to discover that their parents' marriage wasn't really a marriage at all." George agreed. "The Holy Father is tightening up the process to avoid some of the abuses that have crept in."

She read the booklet that evening and wondered why Matthew's exception, which allows divorce in the case of unfaithfulness, was overlooked. But she heard a lot more on the subject the following Tuesday evening when they began to consider:

> *When Jesus had finished these discourses, he left Galilee and came into that part of Judaea which lay beyond the Jordan. And a vast multitude followed him, and he cured them there.*
>
> *Then came some of the Pharisees to him to put him to the proof by the question, "Has a man a right to divorce his wife whenever he chooses?"*

"Have you not read," he replied, "that he who made them made them from the beginning male and female, and said, 'For this reason a man shall leave his father and mother and be united to his wife, and the two shall be one'? Thus they are no longer two, but one! What therefore God has joined together, let not man separate."

"Why then," said they, "did Moses command the husband to give her a written notice of divorce, and so put her away?"

"Moses," he replied, "in consideration of the hardness of your nature permitted you to put away your wives, but it has not been so from the beginning. And I tell you that whoever divorces his wife for any reason except her unfaithfulness, and marries another woman, commits adultery."

Martha was eager to have her say. "We have just been talking about radical forgiveness in Chapter 18 and now we are back into the world of patriarchy and punishment. Do you notice that it is the man's point of view and his rights which are being discussed as though the idea of a woman obtaining divorce from an abusive husband is completely out of the question!" She was only beginning. She went on to relate her own experience as a Roman Catholic in a failed marriage, with a husband who was openly unfaithful and evidently felt no need to apologize. "My parish priest told me that I should pray for him and be an obedient wife!" Webster intervened to cool things off a bit by remarking that Mark's Gospel has essentially the same text but omits the exception for adultery. Melanie said her piece about annulments in the Roman Catholic Church but wished to avoid "Rome-bashing" from Martha or anyone else. Fortunately, things calmed down and Al was helpful in observing that the whole question had a huge literature and recalled his own parents' divorce and the problem that caused for his father in the Anglican Church in Australia. "It seems that churches have widely different policies on the matter. But what about the next bit?" he asked, giving Melanie a cue to proceed:

"If this is the case with a man in relation to his wife," said the disciples to him, "it is better not to marry."

"It is not every man," he replied, "who can receive this teaching, but only those on whom the grace has been bestowed."

"Why do you think the disciples were shocked? Did they all think of marriage as something from which they could easily escape? My reading suggests that divorce in those days was rather easy for men." Too late to recall the last words! Martha was not to be denied as she launched again into her passionate monologue although she ended with an apology as she realized that she had rather gone over the top. They were glad to proceed:

> *"There are men who from their birth have been disabled from marriage, others who have been so disabled by men, and others who have disabled themselves for the sake of the Kingdom of Heaven. He who is able to receive this, let him receive it."*

Webster remarked that the phrase "disabled from marriage" was in the Greek, "eunuchs" and recalled the King James version "There are some eunuchs which were so born from their mother's womb . . ." and gave an argument that the text as shown on the screen gave the true understanding. He also quoted the Catholic Study Bible as giving a helpful translation: *Some are incapable of marriage because they were born so; some, because they were made so by others; some, because they have renounced marriage for the sake of the kingdom of heaven.* He thought that three categories were worth some thought: that some were constitutionally unable to enter into marriage (this might include gay people); others had been made so by experience, maybe abuse; and the third category were those who renounced marriage to become religious celibates. Martha wanted to hold forth on the dangers of compulsory celibacy for priests but she contented herself by saying, "I look forward to a time in my Church when celibacy is an option for priests." It was a relief to encounter a more congenial passage:

> *Then young children were brought to him for him to put his hands on them and pray; but the disciples interfered. Jesus however said, "Let the little children come to me, and do not hinder them; for it is to those who are childlike that the Kingdom of Heaven belongs." So he laid his hands upon them and went away.*

Melanie wondered why another episode commending children was included after they had encountered something very similar in Chapter 18. Stephen commented that this text and others like it are used to justify the practice of infant baptism although he thought it a bit of a stretch. They noticed that, in contrast to Chapter 18, this seemed to be an event rather than a simple piece of teaching; that the disciples needed to have a "learning moment". Perhaps this was the point of the repetition: that the disciples, and by extension, the church needed to learn a lesson. " 'Needs' not 'needed'," remarked Andrew. "We still think of children as second class Christians, cute participants in the Christmas pageant, but otherwise to be excluded from our grownup life."

Then, onwards:

> "Teacher," said one man, coming up to him, "what that is good shall I do in order to win eternal life?"
>
> "Why do you ask me," he replied, "about what is good? There is only One who is truly good. But if you desire to enter into life, keep the commandments."
>
> "Which commandments?" he asked.
>
> Jesus answered, "Thou shalt not kill; Thou shalt not commit adultery; Thou shalt not steal; Thou shalt not lie in giving evidence; Honour thy father and thy mother; and Thou shalt love thy fellow man as much as thyself."
>
> "All of these," said the young man, "I have carefully kept. What do I still lack?"
>
> "If you desire to be perfect," replied Jesus, "go and sell all that you have, and give to the poor, and you shall have wealth in Heaven; and come, follow me."
>
> On hearing those words the young man went away much cast down; for he had much property.
>
> So Jesus said to His disciples, "I solemnly tell you that it is with difficulty that a rich man will enter the Kingdom of Heaven. Yes, I tell you, it is easier for a camel to go through the eye of a needle than for a rich man to enter the Kingdom of God." These words utterly amazed the disciples, and they asked, "Who then can be saved?"
>
> Jesus looked at them and said, "With men this is impossible, but with God everything is possible."

Webster commented the difference between this and the parallel texts in Mark and Luke, where the opening address is "Good teacher," and Jesus replies, "Why call me good; there is none good but God." He remarked, "It seems to me that Matthew's version is a bit awkward. Also Mark contains the detail that "Jesus, looking on him, loved him," which is absent from Matthew." Andrew wondered if this line of thought was useful. "It's part of the discussion about the possible knowledge Matthew had of Mark's Gospel. If we pursue that, then we have to account for each difference between the two. My guess is that this story circulated in various forms." Melanie wanted to direct the discussion towards the meaning of this episode rather than its history but Al had one more piece of information to impart. He had somehow discovered that there was an early Christian writing called *The Gospel according to the Hebrews*. "It's only known because it's quoted by other writers." Al's point was that after Jesus says, "Follow me," there were the additional words, "But the rich man began to scratch his head for it did not please him. And the Lord said to him, 'How can you say, I have fulfilled the Law and the Prophets, when it is written in the Law: You shall love your neighbour as yourself; and, lo, many of your brothers, sons of Abraham, are clothed in filth, dying of hunger, and your house is full of good things, none of which goes out to them'." This gave Melanie the cue to ask about the role of voluntary poverty in the life of that community, and in modern times. Again, Martha had things to say about vows of poverty. "Members of religious communities take vows of poverty, along with celibacy and obedience. But they are economically more secure than almost anyone else in society, with care and comfort from profession to the grave." Melanie worried that this session was becoming a kind of therapy session for Martha but she directed the discussion to the possibility that it was possible to live in a kind of voluntary poverty. "I suppose that the avoidance of wasteful spending and generous actions to those less fortunate might be as far as most of us get." She spoke of the *pro bono* tradition in the legal profession, hoping that this would open up a discussion. Al spoke tactfully. "With all due respect, *pro bono* services might be closer to the crumbs falling from the rich man's table than some approximation to voluntary poverty. But at least it gets people thinking." Melanie thought it would be useful to combine this discussion with a consideration of the remaining text, the disciples' response to the idea of poverty for the sake of the Kingdom:

> *Then Peter said to Jesus, "See, we have forsaken everything and followed you; what then will be our reward?"*
> *"I solemnly tell you," replied Jesus, "that in the new creation, when the Son of Man has taken his seat on his glorious throne,*

all of you who have followed me shall also sit on twelve thrones and judge the twelve tribes of Israel. And whoever has forsaken houses, or brothers or sisters, or father or mother or wife, or children or lands, for my sake, shall receive many times as much and shall have as his inheritance eternal life. But many who are now first will be last, and many who are now last will be first."

Stephen revived his theory about "two documents". He observed that again Peter is the spokesman but drew attention to the rather crass nature of his question. From Andrew came the observation that such a text should put to rest any lingering thought that Jesus was promising some other-worldly kingdom. "It's about as concrete and this-worldly as you can get." Webster observed that the "many times" appears in many manuscripts as "a hundred times" and wondered, impishly, if Peter was ready for a multiplicity of wives and mothers-in-law. "How can we compete against the Islamic promises of 'doe-eyed and ever-willing virgins'?" he asked. But Stephen had the final word. "There is a German scholar who writes under the name 'Christoph Luxenberg'. In 2007, he created a great stir in Islamic studies by producing new understandings of the Koran. In particular, he argues that, instead of 'doe-eyed and ever-willing virgins', the reward for the faithful will be 'white raisins of crystal clarity'. As you can imagine, he must conceal his identity for fear of a *fatwah*!"

Melanie realized that they had rather drifted away from questions about poverty and wondered to herself if this was their way of avoiding a profoundly uncomfortable subject! But it was time to go and she bid them a fond farewell.

Chapter 20

AL AND MELANIE SAT at the same table in the coffee shop where they had met before. He had asked to meet with her, expressing the need for advice. After the usual pleasantries, Al spoke of baptism; he reminded her that, because of his mother's anger towards the church, he had never been baptized. "Now I'm thinking about it," he said, "but there are problems. If it was a question of wanting to identify myself as a follower of Jesus, I believe I am there. Matthew's Gospel has done that for me. But they want much more: that I should be able to affirm my belief in the Apostles' Creed and so on. I'm not sure that I will ever be ready for that." Melanie was silent for a while. "You may be raising this question with the wrong person. We have encountered the text about the blind leading the blind." Al responded that he didn't think of the two of them as blind so much as partially sighted; in such a case, perhaps one leading the other was a good thing. There was another pause and then Al said, "I've been reading an essay by Jack Miles, who was famous recently for his book, 'A History of God.' He's not a Christian in any conventional sense: but he has certainly thought a great deal about faith and community." He pulled out his laptop from his shoulder bag and said, "Do you remember the bit of Schweitzer you showed me? I keep going back to it. Well, here is a bit of Miles which speaks to me."

Melanie read:

> *I can understand the anxiety of those who fear that if the members of a church cannot speak with some confidence of the reality that brings them together, then they cannot presume to speak of anything else. It is this anxiety – in our era, at least – that tends to make faith seem primary, while hope and love seem secondary and derivative. It is this, too, that makes uniformity in the expression of faith, down to individual words and individual letters, seem so crucial. But there may be other ways to build unity and identity.*

> Christian love, as celebrated in the ritual of the Eucharist and enacted in works of mercy, especially if that love is consciously framed by the hope that the ritual and the works are not nonsensical or vain even when they seem so, preserves a space for faith even while leaving that space empty.
>
> For now, is it not enough for Christians to know they are Christians by their love? All the rest need not—indeed must not—be negated, but agreement about it can be indefinitely postponed.

This was new to Melanie and she asked for a copy. "It is clear to me you should be looking for a church constituted around ideas like that," she responded. "Let me know when you find one! And, by the way, he speaks of faith, hope and love. Doesn't St. Paul talk about these three and end up with the verdict, 'The greatest of these is love.' And Paul wasn't reluctant to press the claims of faith!" Al sighed and found solace in his latte. "What to do?" he lamented. "It is tempting to just conform to what the church asks and find some interpretation of the baptismal promises which I can live with." Melanie surprised herself by suggesting that the church was generous in its dealings with those who were overly scrupulous.

She went away, unaccountably anxious and was restless for the remainder of the day. She was cheered with the reading of Chapter 20. If God is to be understood as unreasonably generous, maybe some of his people will show similar characteristics!

She was eager to proceed as they gathered and wondered if Al would draw conclusions from the first section:

> "For the Kingdom of Heaven is like an employer who went out early in the morning to hire men to work in his vineyard, and having made an agreement with them for a dollar a day, sent them into his vineyard. About nine o'clock he went out and saw others loitering in the market-place. To these also he said, 'You also, go into the vineyard, and whatever is right I will give you.' So they went. Again about twelve, and about three o'clock, he went out and did the same. And going out about five o'clock he found others loitering, and he asked them, 'Why have you been standing here all day long, doing nothing?' 'Because no one has hired us,' they replied. 'You also, go into the vineyard,' he said. When eve-

> ning came, the master said to his steward, 'Call the men and pay them their wages. Begin with the last set and finish with the first.'
>
> When those came who had begun at five o'clock, they received a dollar apiece and when the first came, they expected to get more, but they also each got the dollar. So when they had received it, they grumbled against the employer, saying, 'These who came last have done only one hour's work, and you have put them on a level with us who have worked the whole day and have borne the scorching heat.'
>
> 'My friend,' he answered to one of them, 'I am doing you no injustice. Did you not agree with me for a dollar? Take your money and go. I choose to give this last comer just as much as I give you. Have I not a right to do what I choose with my own property? Or are you envious because I am generous?'
>
> So the last shall be first, and the first last."

Melanie commented that she had replaced the word, "shilling," in the Weymouth text she had inherited, with the word, "dollar," as a reminder of the millions in the modern world whose income did not exceed a dollar a day. Webster, ever helpful, recalled the word "penny" from the King James version and "denarius" from other modern translations. Andrew remarked, "I've read interpretations that Gentiles were the latecomers and that this parable was a product of the early church, wishing to establish their equality." Melanie reminded the group of their discussion about parable interpretation earlier and proposed that the parable might be about the generosity of God, especially to those who live, literally from hand to mouth. Trying not to glance at Al, she repeated her hope that the church could be as generous to latecomers.

Stephen was quick to compare this with the Parable of the Sower. "In both cases," he said, "the protagonist apparently acts against his own best interests." As a final comment, Al said, "So much of this is congenial and makes me want to live with it. I have been wondering what Christianity might look like if we had only Matthew as our Holy Book!" They were silent but eventually agreed that it would look very different.

Melanie was planning to comment about the last verse ("the first will be last and the last will be first") and to point out that it seemed out of place. And that it had already appeared in Chapter 19, in a more logical place, but she kept quiet. It was a moment to treasure. After another silence, she placed before them the third passion prediction:

> Jesus was now going up to Jerusalem, and he took the twelve disciples aside by themselves, and on the way he said to them, "We are going up to Jerusalem, and there the Son of Man will be betrayed to the High Priests and Scribes. They will condemn him to death, and hand him over to the Gentiles to be made sport of and scourged and crucified; and on the third day he will be raised to life."

They noticed that, for the first time, crucifixion and resurrection are mentioned and that, in contrast to the earlier predictions, no response from the disciples is recorded. Andrew thought that this was a deliberate choice by Matthew, to underline the inability to face the horror of the prospect before them. The prediction of the resurrection scarcely would register in the face of the overwhelming horror associated with the very thought of crucifixion. "Instead of a response, he follows such a solemn moment with a piece of crass behavior on the part of the disciples. That says something about Matthew, perhaps."

Melanie obligingly moved the text forward:

> Then the mother of the sons of Zebedee came to him with her sons, and knelt before him to make a request of him. "What is it you desire?" he asked. "Command," she replied, "that these my two sons may sit one at your right hand and one at your left in your Kingdom."
>
> "None of you know what you are asking for," said Jesus; "can you drink out of the cup from which I am about to drink?"
>
> "We can," they replied. "You shall drink out of my cup," he said, "but a seat at my right hand or at my left it is not for me to allot, but it belongs to those for whom it has been prepared by my Father." The other ten heard of this, and their indignation was aroused against the two brothers. But Jesus called them to him, and said, "You know that the rulers of the Gentiles lord it over them, and their great men exercise authority over them. Not so shall it be among you; but whoever desires to be great among you shall be your servant, and whoever desires to be first among you shall be your bondservant; just as the Son of Man came not to be served but to serve, and to give His life as the redemption-price for many."

Webster observed that Mark has the same episode but has James and John, the sons of Zebedee make the approach. "It looks like this has been tampered with to protect the reputation of the two disciples. Look at the subsequent conversation, addressed to James and John. Their mother disappears entirely."

It was time for Martha again. "Blame Mother, it's happened before. And will happen again," she said with some bitterness. But Stephen wanted to tackle the text. "Where did the idea of the cup of suffering originate?" he asked. "I know that the imagery is used in the Old Testament but always as a symbol of God's wrath. Surely Jesus didn't think that what he was going to endure was because of God's anger." Andrew suggested that the anger was not directed towards Jesus but towards those who reject him. "I have heard the text from Isaiah about his death: ' . . . wounded for our transgressions, bruised for our iniquities . . . ' Maybe there is a hint of that already."

Webster, on the other hand, wished to think about the purported willingness of the disciples to share in suffering. "I once heard a preacher say, 'As you share in the communion cup, think of the challenge, 'Are you able to drink from the cup from which I am about to drink?' That saying rather haunts me at the communion rail." This brought about an unexpected digression. Al said, "Some of you will know that I am not baptized and that question has to be settled sooner or later. But in the mean time, on those rare occasions when I go to church, should I receive communion?" Melanie didn't want this to become a counseling group for Al but allowed the general discussion to reach an inconclusive end. "Perhaps we can continue this when we discuss the Last Supper in a week or two. Meantime, let's keep an eye on the clock." Using this as justification, she advanced to the final section of Chapter 20:

> *As they were leaving Jericho, an immense crowd following him, two blind men sitting by the roadside heard that it was Jesus who was passing by, and cried aloud, "Sir, Son of David, pity us." The people angrily tried to silence them, but they cried all the louder. "O Sir, Son of David, pity us," they said.*
>
> *So Jesus stood still and called to them. "What shall I do for you?" he asked. "Sir, let our eyes be opened," they replied. Moved with compassion, Jesus touched their eyes, and immediately they regained their sight and followed him.*

Anticipating Webster, she noted that Luke has one unnamed blind man, Mark adds the name, "Bartimaeus" and now Matthew loses the name but doubles the number. "A suggestion, I think, that this story circulated in several forms." Andrew commented that the phrase translated, "Sir, pity us," in the Greek, is the familiar "Kyrie eleison" and that this is the only place where this phrase occurs in exactly this way. "I think of this when I say or sing the Kyrie in church, that it was originally a cry for healing rather than forgiveness." This gave rise to an animated discussion of the relation between healing and forgiveness with the conclusion that they weren't very different after all.

And the conclusion that it was a good time to depart.

Chapter 21

On Wednesday, Melanie received an email from Al with the news that his father in Australia had died and that he was already on his way home for the funeral. She knew that Al had been raised by his mother and that he had had little contact with his father, the Archdeacon. She sent a reply expressing regrets that he would have this ordeal to face and assuring him that he would be much missed by the group. In immediate reply, he asked for an update on the coming Tuesday meeting and hoped that he would be back the following week and only miss one. She realized in a new way that Tuesdays and Matthew's Gospel had become important to them both. "Is Aunt Matty chuckling?" she wondered.

By Saturday evening, she had another message (by then it was Sunday in Australia). The service on Saturday had been conducted by the Bishop in the Cathedral with a large crowd attending, including many clergy. Al's mother, however, decided not to be present and this obviously was painful for Al. He spoke positively of the service and the tributes offered by various colleagues of his father. It was a service which included Holy Communion and Al related his difficulty in knowing whether he should receive the sacrament. "I was all ready to feel excluded but there was this one prayer which suggested otherwise. You may know it. It has some reflection of the passage we were studying about the woman who came for healing and spoke of the crumbs falling even to the little puppies under the table. So I decided that if 'little puppies' were in, then there should be a place for me. I received communion for the first time in my life." Melanie took some time to track down the prayer Al had mentioned. "We are not worthy to come to this Thy table trusting in our own righteousness but in Thy plenteous and great mercy. We are not worthy to gather up the crumbs under your table but you are the same Lord whose property is always to have mercy . . ."

During the next few days, she wondered what was happening to Al, but was soon preoccupied with work at the office and preparation for Tuesday.

She was soon aware that Matthew's narrative was now beginning its final phase: that of the days in Jerusalem before the Passion began. They had all done their homework and had picked up the sense of the gathering storm and their somber mood was intensified by the news of Al's journey to his homeland. And so they began:

> *When they were come near Jerusalem and had arrived at Bethphage and the Mount of Olives, Jesus sent two of the disciples on in front, saying to them, "Go to the village you see facing you, and as you enter it you will find a she-ass tied up and a foal with her. Untie her and bring them to me. And if any one says anything to you, say, 'The Master needs them,' and he will at once send them."*
>
> *This took place in order that the prophet's prediction might be fulfilled:*
>
> *"Tell the Daughter of Zion, 'See, thy King is coming to thee, gentle, and yet mounted on an ass, even on a colt the foal of an ass.'"*
>
> *So the disciples went and did as Jesus had instructed them: they brought the she-ass and the foal, and threw their outer garments on them. So he sat on them; and most of the crowd kept spreading their garments along the road, while others cut branches from the trees and carpeted the road with them, and the multitudes—some of the people preceding him and some following—sang aloud, "God save the Son of David! Blessings on him who comes in the Lord's name! God in the highest Heavens save him!"*
>
> *When he thus entered Jerusalem, the whole city was thrown into commotion, every one inquiring, "Who is this?"*
>
> *"This is Jesus, the Prophet, from Nazareth in Galilee," replied the crowds.*

Webster was quick to remind them that the idea of the two animals was due to a misunderstanding on the part of Matthew. The text from Zechariah is an instance of the way Hebrew poetry used parallel statements; the other Gospels avoid the rather ludicrous image of Jesus riding two animals at once! But they quickly passed on to a more substantive discussion. They thought about Palm Sunday as they experienced it in church, with processions and palm branches. Stephen had an interesting observation. "Why don't we focus more on the spreading of garments? After all, this would involve a real sacrifice, you might literally lose your shirt. And the shedding of the outer garment might suggest a willingness to part with our protective shell!" There was general enthusiasm for the idea and Andrew, who was a member of the worship committee of his church, promised to raise this suggestion for Palm Sunday worship. There were various comical suggestions about shedding of garments as part of the liturgy!

Andrew also was interested to explore the question of whether the willingness of the owner to part with his ass was the result of some previous arrangement or a miraculous happening. There was general agreement that the first option was more likely. Martha commented that they were still uncomfortable with the miraculous except when some human life or well being was at stake. "That's why we all were so uneasy about the coin in the mouth of the fish in Chapter 17."

Webster wondered if this demonstration of kingship, even of a very humble kind, was the beginning of political trouble. "The Romans did not look kindly on anyone who gave a hint of revolutionary kingship. They knew how easily things could get out of hand. No doubt some Roman bureaucrat opened a new file that day, headed 'Jesus bar Joseph, Nazareth, potential troublemaker.' Who could have dreamed that the followers of this odd character would overthrow the Empire!"

Then onwards to the Cleansing of the Temple.

> *Entering the Temple, Jesus drove out all who were buying and selling there, and overturned the money-changers' tables and the seats of the pigeon-dealers.*
>
> *"It is written," he said, " 'My House shall be called the House of Prayer', but you are making it a robbers' cave." And the blind and the lame came to him in the Temple, and he cured them.*
>
> *But when the High Priests and the Scribes saw the wonderful things that he had done and the children who were crying aloud in the Temple, "God save the Son of David," they were filled with indignation.*
>
> *"Do you hear," they asked him, "what these children are saying?"*
>
> *"Yes," he replied; "have you never read, 'Out of the mouths of infants and of babes at the breast Thou hast brought forth the praise which is due'?"*
>
> *So he left them and went out of the city to Bethany and passed the night there.*

Stephen, apparently taking Al's place as proponent of original ideas, said, "Here he goes. First get the Romans suspicious and then offend the religious establishment. If this was an ordinary piece of history, you might say this man had a death wish!" This provoked a vigorous debate: was Jesus deliberately trying to provoke the powers-that-be? It was not unknown that a prophet might try to arrange for the fulfillment of his own prophecies. What was in his mind? Perhaps the act of offering himself up would bring God's intervention and the inauguration of the Kingdom. Webster had anticipated that this discussion would arise earlier rather than later and he had arranged with Melanie that the famous quote from Albert Schweitzer might be displayed:

> *There is silence all around. The Baptist appears, and cries: "Repent, for the Kingdom of Heaven is at hand." Soon after that comes Jesus, and, in the knowledge that He is the coming Son of Man, lays hold of the wheel of the world to set it moving on that last revolution which is to bring all ordinary history to a close. It refuses to turn, and He throws Himself upon it. Then it does turn; and crushes Him. Instead of bringing in the eschatological conditions, He has destroyed them. The wheel rolls onward, and the mangled body of the one immeasurably great Man, who was strong enough to think of Himself as the spiritual ruler of mankind and to bend history to His purpose, is hanging upon it still. That is His victory and His reign.*

They read this with some astonishment. "Is this saying that Jesus essentially committed suicide?" asked Andrew. Webster would only say that he thought that Schweitzer's idea should be known, however bizarre it might seem to those brought up with conventional theology. Martha had encountered Dorothy Sayers, "The Man Born to be King" in college and outlined its line that the betrayal which Judas plots was designed to force Jesus to show his kingly powers and bring in the Kingdom. Melanie was somewhat surprised that this discussion had continued and thought that, on the whole, it had opened up the field for the future. Questions about the meaning of the Crucifixion were going to come sooner or later.

With an eye on the clock, she pushed ahead:

> *Early in the morning as he was on his way to return to the city he was hungry, and seeing a fig-tree on the road-side he went up to it, but found nothing on it but leaves. "On you," he said, "no fruit shall ever again grow." And immediately the fig tree withered away.*

> *When the disciples saw it they exclaimed in astonishment, "How instantaneously the fig-tree has withered away!"*
>
> *"I solemnly tell you," said Jesus, "that if you have an unwavering faith, you shall not only perform such a miracle as this of the fig-tree, but that even if you say to this mountain, 'Be thou lifted up and hurled into the sea,' it shall be done; and everything, whatever it be, that you ask for in your prayers, if you have faith, you shall obtain."*

"How strange," said Andrew, "that such an odd bit of business would be inserted here. I suppose it could be seen as a parable acted out." Webster wanted to remind them that the fig tree was a symbol of Israel and that its state of leafiness without fruit might be another way in which Jesus expresses his hostility against the leadership of the nation.

They recognized that the saying about hurling the mountain into the sea had occurred before but in a different form: in Chapter 17, faith like a grain of mustard would suffice; now it's "unwavering faith". And the effectiveness of prayer is related to faith. Stephen was impatient. "I can't wait for next year when Melanie guides us to an understanding of prayer," he said in his teasing fashion. "So I've been looking at what we have encountered to date. Early, the Sermon on the Mount and its unblushing promises, 'ask and you'll get' and then Chapter 17, as we have just mentioned with faith as a grain of mustard seed as a condition. But don't forget Chapter 18, where 'two of you must agree' and prayers will be answered. Now this." But Andrew was comfortable with the conditional promises. "They aren't necessarily contradictory but perhaps give different conditions under which prayers will be answered. I have more problems with the unconditional promises." Melanie needed to suggest that if Stephen was so interested in this subject, then he might think of taking over the following year. They exchanged ironic glances.

So next:

> *He entered the Temple; and while he was teaching, the High Priests and the Elders of the people came to him and asked him, "By what authority are you doing these things? and who gave you this authority?"*
>
> *"And I also have a question to ask you," replied Jesus, "and if you answer me, I in turn will tell you by what authority I do these things. John's Baptism, whence was it? - had it a heavenly or a human origin?" So they debated the matter among themselves "If we*

say 'a heavenly origin'," they argued, "he will say, 'Why then did you not believe him?' and if we say 'a human origin' we have the people to fear, for they all hold John to have been a Prophet."

So they answered Jesus, "We do not know."

"Nor do I tell you," He replied, "by what authority I do these things."

"But give me your judgement. There was a man who had two sons. He came to the elder of them, and said, 'My son, go and work in the vineyard to-day.'

'I will not,' he replied. But afterwards he was sorry, and went.

He came to the second and spoke in the same manner. His answer was, 'I will go, Sir.' But he did not go. Which of the two did as his father desired?"

"The first," they said. "I solemnly tell you," replied Jesus, "that the tax-gatherers and the notorious sinners are entering the Kingdom of God in front of you.

For John came to you observing all sorts of ritual, and you put no faith in him: the tax-gatherers and the notorious sinners did put faith in him, and you, though you saw this example set you, were not even afterwards sorry so as to believe him."

"So, here was this upstart from the boonies," said Stephen. "It was time to put him in his place." Webster endorsed the idea that Galilee might qualify as the "boonies". He had read somewhere that not only did Galileans speak with an upcountry accent, a fact that would contribute to Peter's denial later, but they were thought to be contaminated by the contact with Gentiles who had colonized the region. "The text suggests that Jesus immediately went on the offensive and rather put his visitors in their place, or rather, in a place they would prefer to avoid." They agreed that Jesus "won the battle but lost the war," speaking from a secular perspective. Powerful authorities do not relish such a public humiliation. "Even more than the cleansing of the temple, this would be unforgivable," said Andrew. "And the parable which Matthew records next, if it was also spoken in the same setting, would rub salt in the wound." Melanie was always grateful for a cue to move on and so she showed:

> He told them another parable: "A man planted a vineyard, made a fence round it, dug a wine-tank in it, and built a strong lodge; then let the place to vine-dressers, and went abroad. When

> *vintage-time approached, he sent his servants to the vine-dressers to receive his share of the grapes; but the vine-dressers seized the servants, and one they cruelly beat, one they killed, one they pelted with stones. Again he sent another party of servants more numerous than the first; and these they treated in the same manner. Later still he sent to them his son, saying, 'They will respect my son.' But the vine-dressers, when they saw the son, said to one another, 'Here is the heir: come, let us kill him and get his inheritance.' So they seized him, dragged him out of the vineyard, and killed him. When then the owner of the vineyard comes, what will he do to those vine-dressers?"*
>
> *"He will put the wretches to a wretched death," was the reply, "and will entrust the vineyard to other vine-dressers who will render the produce to him at the vintage season."*
>
> *"Have you never read in the Scriptures," said Jesus, " 'The stone which the builders rejected has been made the cornerstone: this cornerstone came from the Lord, and is wonderful in our eyes'? That, I tell you, is the reason why the Kingdom of God will be taken away from you, and given to a nation that will exhibit the power of it. He who falls on this stone will be severely hurt; but he on whom it falls will be utterly crushed."*
>
> *After listening to His parables the High Priests and the Pharisees perceived that he was speaking about them; but though they were eager to lay hands upon him, they were afraid of the people, for by them he was regarded as a prophet.*

They all agreed that the symbolism of the vineyard was a clear linkage to Israel; Andrew could even quote the Song of the Vineyard from Isaiah 5: *The vineyard of the Lord Almighty is the house of Israel and the men of Judah are the garden of his delight. And he looked for justice but saw bloodshed; for righteousness, but heard cries of distress.* But Melanie, having gone back to Jeremias, observed that a different version of this parable was known to the early church. From the Gospel of Thomas she was able to display:

> *A good man had a vineyard. He gave it to some farmers so that they would work it and he would receive its profits from them. He sent his servant so that the farmers would give him the profits of the vineyard. They seized his servant, they beat him and almost*

> killed him. The servant went back; he told his master. The master said, "Perhaps he was unknown to them." He sent another servant. The farmers beat the other one. Then the master sent his son. He said, "Perhaps they will respect my son." Those farmers seized him, they killed him, since he was the heir to the vineyard.

Andrew was quick to comment. "I don't get it. It seems much the same as Matthew's version, just simpler." Melanie replied, "That was my first reaction, too. Jeremias says that the original meaning was a vindication of the offer of the gospel to the poor. 'You tenants of the vineyard, you leaders of the people! ... You have rebelled against God. Therefore the vineyard of God shall be given to others.' Jeremias claims that Matthew took this simple parable and heightened the details so that it traced the history of Israel's dealings with the prophets and anticipated the death of Jesus." All seemed genuinely puzzled. Melanie could only remark that it seemed that scholars like Jeremias were dead set against allegorical interpretation; she tried to make it clear that she was merely reporting what she had read!

On this rather confusing note, they agreed to end the session. As they left, Melanie fell in step with Stephen, thanking him for the comments he had made and assuring him that the agenda for the following year was open. "It may be that this is the end of 'Matty's Meetings,'" she remarked. "Not 'Matty's Meetings' but 'Melanie's Meetings' from now on," he replied. "Don't count on it," was her reply.

Returning home, she sent a long email to Al, reviewing the evening's discussion and remarking that he was needed "to keep them honest." She wondered how his experiences in Australia would have affected him.

Chapter 22

THAT EVENING, MELANIE FOUND herself thinking alternatively about Al's absence in Australia which had altered the chemistry of the group and also fretting a bit over her second opportunity to explain the ideas of Jeremias about the interpretation of parables. She realized she didn't really grasp the reason for his insistence that allegorical interpretations were to be avoided at all cost. She knew that allegory could lead to wild interpretations. Somewhere she had read of an interpretation of the parable of the Good Samaritan in which, as she remembered it, the oil and wine used for the wounds of the victim are the sacraments of Baptism and Eucharist, the inn is the church and the innkeeper, the head of the Church, maybe the Pope, and the promise that the Samaritan will return is the second coming of Christ. She could see how imaginative people might come up with bizarre interpretations. But she fretted over the coming chapter with its big parable at the beginning. She thought that the debates Jesus had with opponents would be more manageable.

So the days passed without incident until it was Tuesday again. She had had no further contact with Al and hesitated, for reasons which were a bit obscure, even to herself, to email him.

The gathering was ready and she began by asking that they avoided another debate about the interpretation of parables. "I have tried to explain the views of Jeremias twice and now I realize that I don't fully understand them myself." They seemed content with this and so they considered:

> *Again Jesus spoke to them in parables.*
> *"The Kingdom of Heaven," he said, "may be compared to a king who celebrated the marriage of his son, and sent his servants to call the invited guests to the wedding, but they were unwilling to come. Again he sent other servants with a message to those who were invited. 'My breakfast is now ready,' he said, 'my bullocks and fat cattle are killed, and every preparation is made: come to*

the wedding.' They however gave no heed, but went, one to his home in the country, another to his business; and the rest seized the king's servants, maltreated them, and murdered them. So the king's anger was stirred, and he sent his troops and destroyed those murderers and burnt their city. Then he said to his servants, 'The wedding banquet is ready, but those who were invited were unworthy of it. Go out therefore to the crossroads, and everybody you meet invite to the wedding.'

So they went out into the roads and gathered together all they could find, both bad and good, and the banqueting hall was filled with guests.

Now the king came in to see the guests; and among them he discovered one who was not wearing a wedding-robe.

'My friend,' he said, 'how is it that you came in here without a wedding robe?' The man stood speechless. Then the king said to the servants,

'Bind him hand and foot and fling him into the darkness outside: there will be the weeping aloud and the gnashing of teeth.'

For there are many called, but few chosen."

There was general agreement that this story seemed rather over the top. Stephen wanted a moment of sympathy for the cooks, called to keep the banquet on hold while the army was out burning a city and murdering its inhabitants. "And if that wasn't enough, the dinner needed further delay as the town's ne'er-do-wells were gathered up." Webster reminded them of Luke's version of the parable with its much gentler, less melodramatic approach: a man, not a King, gives a feast, not a marriage banquet; the invited guests make excuses but there is no violence, let alone the burning of a city. And most notable of all, no sign of the closing episode about the guest without the wedding garment. Martha had something to say about the last part. "It seems preposterous that anyone who has been gathered in from the street would have time to rush home to change. I have the feeling that this last part is an addition and I think I know why it was added," she said. "The early church, just like us, found it hard to deal with the radical inclusiveness of the original teaching of Jesus. So there was the need for the wedding garment, which might represent any number of things. Something is demanded so that we qualify for the

Kingdom. Baptism, maybe, or good works or both. That's what preachers usually insist it means." She spoke with some intensity.

Melanie was thinking of Al's experience of "radical inclusiveness" when he took communion at his father's funeral but knew that it would be inappropriate to share this confidence. Instead she said, "Do you remember that two weeks ago Al asked what Christianity might look like if we only had Matthew's Gospel? My guess is that it would be a good deal more inclusive and that we wouldn't have the struggles over the role of women and same-sex blessings." This led to a rather heated discussion which Melanie could quell only by moving forward to:

> *Then the Pharisees went and consulted together how they might entrap him in his conversation. So they sent to him their disciples together with the Herodians, who said, "Teacher, we know that you are truthful and that you faithfully teach God's truth; and that no fear of man misleads you, for you are not biased by men's wealth or rank. Give us your judgement therefore: is it allowable for us to pay a poll-tax to Caesar, or not?" Perceiving their wickedness, Jesus replied, "Why are you hypocrites trying to ensnare me? Show me the coin." And they brought him a tribute coin.*
>
> *"Whose likeness and inscription," he asked, "is this?"*
>
> *"Caesar's," they replied.*
>
> *"Pay therefore," he rejoined, "what is Caesar's to Caesar; and what is God's to God."*
>
> *They heard this, and were astonished; then left him, and went their way.*

She could remind them that the remainder of the chapter consisted of three challenges from various hostile parties. They were a succession of trick questions, designed to make a country preacher stumble. For the tribute question as displayed, Stephen remarked the manner in which Jesus again answered a question by proposing another question. "Just as he did when they asked about his authority in Chapter 21." They debated the meaning of the famous answer, whether it meant that all money belonged to Caesar. Stephen asked, "Does this mean that he was urging upon his followers a total indifference to money?" But Webster wondered if the cryptic response was simply a case of Jesus responding in kind. "It is a part of a rhetorical game, perhaps, with Jesus showing his mastery of the situation. But he has left us to debate what he meant.

Is this the beginning of the 'separation of church and state'?" Martha wished to draw attention to the historic "Peace Churches," Quakers, Mennonites and others, whose members object to their taxes being used for military purposes. She mentioned the long history of such efforts and the fact that in Canada in the eighteen forties, it was possible for Christians of those persuasions to divert taxes from military purposes to public works. It seemed that such convictions were based, at least in part, on the answer Jesus gave. "But many other Christians have drawn very different conclusions," she conceded.

Then the next test, coming from a different quarter:

> On the same day a party of Sadducees came to him, contending that there is no resurrection. And they put this case to him: "Teacher," they said, "Moses enjoined, 'If a man die childless, his brother shall marry his widow, and raise up a family for him.' Now we had among us seven brothers. The eldest of them married, but died childless, leaving his wife to his brother. So also did the second and the third, down to the seventh till the woman also died, after surviving them all. At the Resurrection, therefore, whose wife of the seven will she be? for they all married her."
>
> The reply of Jesus was, "You are in error, through ignorance of the Scriptures and of the power of God. For in the Resurrection, men neither marry nor are women given in marriage, but they are like angels in Heaven. But as to the Resurrection of the dead, have you never read what God says to you, 'I am the God of Abraham, the God of Isaac, and the God of Jacob'? He is not the God of the dead, but of the living."
>
> All the crowd heard this, and were filled with amazement at his teaching.

Andrew had gone to some trouble to read up on the distinction between the Pharisees and the Sadducees since the two groups had previously been spoken of together. "Two major differences," he said. "Firstly, the Sadducees came from the upper classes and the priesthood while Pharisees were often men of humble origin. But more importantly, there was the major theological difference, that the Sadducees held to a strict interpretation of the Torah while the Pharisees accepted the subsequent teachings as authoritative." Melanie was grateful that he didn't go on any further. She knew how difficult it was to condense an hour's reading into a few sentences. Stephen was quick with a question. "If the Sadducees were so keen on the written word of Scripture, how was it that they denied the resurrection? They must have known the book of Daniel in which it is said, 'Multitudes who sleep in the dust of the earth will awake: some to everlasting life, others to shame and everlasting contempt.' This would seem clear enough." No one could answer but Andrew supposed that they only accepted the Pentateuch, the five books of Moses. No one had read anything to clarify the matter so they went on to discuss the strange question proposed to Jesus. "What was their motive?" asked Webster. "To discredit the idea of resurrection by showing how it led to an impossible situation; or to discredit Jesus?" Someone suggested that maybe they wished to do both. "In any case," said Melanie, "the answer given is not very comforting to those who look forward to a life in the hereafter where they are reunited with loved ones, in particular, with spouses." Martha quoted an example of a widower whom she knew, who was greatly troubled by this answer. " 'If I am not reunited with my dear wife,' he said, 'it won't be Heaven for me.'"

Stephen, in mischievous mood, reminded them of Chapter 19 with its promise that those who left their wives for the sake of Jesus will receive a hundred fold in the life hereafter. "And a hundred mothers-in-law, too," he suggested. He also wondered about the quotation from the book of Exodus: "I am the God of Abraham, Isaac and Jacob," and the inference which Jesus drew from this. "Surely it is not a very convincing argument for resurrection. If God is 'not the God of the dead but the living,' surely this implies that Abraham, Isaac and Jacob are still living, an argument for some kind of immortality of the soul rather than resurrection. I must be missing something here!" If he was missing something, then so were they all and the conversation drifted into discussions of various theories of the afterlife until Melanie, as ever, conscious of the time, moved them along to the final section of the chapter:

> *Now the Pharisees came up when they heard that he had silenced the Sadducees, and one of them, an expounder of the Law, asked him as a test question, "Teacher, which is the greatest Commandment in the Law?"*
>
> *"Thou shalt love the Lord thy God," he answered, "with thy whole heart, thy whole soul, thy whole mind. This is the greatest and foremost Commandment. And the second is similar to it: Thou*

shalt love thy fellow man as much as thyself. The whole of the Law and the Prophets is summed up in these two Commandments."

While the Pharisees were still assembled there, Jesus put a question to them. "What think you about the Christ," He said, "whose son is He?"

"David's," they replied. "How then," he asked, "does David, taught by the Spirit, call Him Lord, when he says, 'The Lord said to my Lord, sit at My right hand until I have put thy foes beneath thy feet' ? If therefore David calls Him Lord, how can He be his son?"

No one could say a word in reply, nor from that day did any one venture again to put a question to him.

Webster was quick to point out that Luke's gospel had the same episode but in a very different context. In Luke, the 'expounder of the Law' asks his question but Jesus replies, " What do you read in the Law?" The questioner then gives the familiar summary of the Law but goes on to ask another question, "Who then is my neighbour?" Then follows the Parable of the Good Samaritan.

No one wished to comment on this piece of information but rather to remark on the way in which Jesus was willing to play their game by asking a question of his own which apparently baffled his opponents. "Well, it baffles me, too," said Stephen. "Maybe Jesus was teasing them!" This was an idea which gave rise to some animated debate. Could they incorporate into their idea of Jesus some thought that he was capable of this kind of thing. Stephen ended the discussion by remarking that if we think of Jesus as truly human, we might expect that he sometimes could be less than totally serious in what he said. This gave them something to think about. Had they missed this possibility in their earlier discussions?

It was time to go and they departed thinking that their ideas of Jesus might require some adjustment.

Chapter 23

Returning home that evening, Melanie was ready to send another email to Al, summarizing the discussions of the group. But already, a message was waiting for her from Al, explaining that he had needed to spend more time in Australia than he had intended, tidying up his father's estate. He was already on his way back and she decided that she would be able to report the progress through Chapter 22 in person.

She also worried about Chapter 23, which now needed to be confronted with its long series of condemnations against the Pharisees. It seemed so excessive; maybe Jesus said all these things at various times and Matthew gathered them into one continuous text.

When the group met, Al was anxious to share some of his experiences even though this ran contrary to their usual practice. But Melanie was content to let him have the floor for a while especially in view of the forthcoming Chapter 23.

He shared some of those same matters he had previously mentioned in his email: his situation in St Peter's Cathedral, Adelaide at his Dad's memorial service, his uncertainty about taking communion and his memories of the "little puppies" from Chapter 15. Andrew responded by reviewing some of their discussions about "radical inclusiveness," the phrase which Martha had introduced at their last session and their subsequent thoughts about the interpretation of the Parable of the Wedding Feast. Not everyone was entirely happy with Andrew's account of their discussions and so Al received a variety of opinions on this matter. But the question was put to him by Stephen. "Do you think of that experience of taking communion as a one-off or do you see yourself now in a different way?" There was a bit of a hush as obviously some thought that Stephen had gone a bit far. But Al put everyone at ease by saying, "Stephen, I remember remarks you made earlier about your baptism. I can be open with you, too. At this stage, I am in a state of confusion. If someone were to ask me whether I saw myself as a Christian, I am not sure what I would say. Certainly, this experience of Matthew's gospel has opened up a whole lot of new possibilities."

Melanie decided that it was time to bite the bullet and to move on. She thanked Al for his openness and spoke of her apprehension about the chapter to be discussed that evening. "It's hard to find much to say about it. Evidently it is a collection of remarks that Jesus was supposed to have uttered. Maybe some of them reflect the hostility between the early church and Pharisaic Judaism. Most of us have learned that after the destruction of Jerusalem in the year 70, the Pharisees became the dominant group in Judaism."

She went on to say that she would put the whole chapter up at once. "Let's get it over with!"

> *Then Jesus addressed the crowds and his disciples.*
>
> *"The Scribes," he said, "and the Pharisees sit in the chair of Moses. Therefore do and observe everything that they command you; but do not imitate their lives, for though they tell others what to do, they do not do it themselves. Heavy and cumbrous burdens they bind together and load men's shoulders with them, while as for themselves, not with one finger do they choose to lift them. And everything they do they do with a view to being observed by men; for they widen their phylacteries and make the tassels large, and love the best seats at a dinner party or in the synagogues, and like to be bowed to in places of public resort, and to be addressed by men as 'Rabbi.'*
>
> *As for you, do not accept the title of 'Rabbi,' for one alone is your Teacher, and you are all brothers. And call no one on earth your Father, for One alone is your Father—the Heavenly Father.*
>
> *And do not accept the name of 'leader,' for your Leader is one alone—the Christ. He who is the greatest among you shall be your servant; and one who exalts himself shall be abased, while one who abases himself shall be exalted.*
>
> *But alas for you, Scribes and Pharisees, hypocrites, for you lock the door of the Kingdom of the Heavens against men; you yourselves do not enter, nor do you allow those to enter who are seeking to do so.*
>
> *Alas for you, Scribes and Pharisees, hypocrites, for you scour sea and land in order to win one convert—and when he is gained, you make him twice as much a son of Gehenna as yourselves.*

Alas for you, you blind guides, who say, 'Whoever swears by the Sanctuary it is nothing; but whoever swears by the gold of the Sanctuary, is bound by the oath.' Blind fools! Why, which is greater?—the gold, or the Sanctuary which has made the gold holy? And you say, 'Whoever swears by the altar, it is nothing; but whoever swears by the offering lying on it is bound by the oath.' You are blind! Why, which is greater?—the offering, or the altar which makes the offering holy? He who swears by the altar swears both by it and by everything on it; he who swears by the Sanctuary swears both by it and by Him who dwells in it; and he who swears by Heaven swears both by the throne of God and by Him who sits upon it.

Alas for you, Scribes and Pharisees, hypocrites, for you pay the tithe on mint, dill, and cumin, while you have neglected the weightier requirements of the Law—just judgement, mercy, and faithful dealing. These things you ought to have done, and yet you ought not to have left the others undone.

You blind guides, straining out the gnat while you gulp down the camel!

Alas for you, Scribes and Pharisees, hypocrites, for you wash clean the outside of the cup or dish, while within they are full of greed and self-indulgence. Blind Pharisees, first wash clean the inside of the cup or dish, and then the outside will be clean also.

Alas for you, Scribes and Pharisees, hypocrites, for you are just like whitewashed sepulchres, the outside of which pleases the eye, though inside they are full of dead men's bones and of all that is unclean.

The same is true of you: outwardly you seem to the human eye to be good and honest men, but, within, you are full of insincerity and disregard of God's Law.

Alas for you, Scribes and Pharisees, hypocrites, for you repair the sepulchres of the Prophets and keep in order the tombs of the righteous, and your boast is, 'If we had lived in the time of our forefathers, we should not have been implicated with them in the murder of the Prophets.'

So that you bear witness against yourselves that you are descendants of those who murdered the Prophets. Fill up the measure of your forefathers' guilt. O serpents, O vipers' brood, how are you to escape condemnation to Gehenna?

> *For this reason I am sending to you Prophets and wise men and Scribes. Some of them you will put to death—nay, crucify; some of them you will flog in your synagogues and chase from town to town that all the innocent blood shed upon earth may come on you, from the blood of righteous Abel to the blood of Zechariah the son of Berechiah whom you murdered between the Sanctuary and the altar.*
>
> *I tell you in solemn truth that all these things will come upon the present generation.*
>
> *O Jerusalem, Jerusalem! You who murder the Prophets and stone those who have been sent to you! How often have I desired to gather thy children to me, just as a hen gathers her chickens under her wings, and you would not come! See, your house will now be left to you desolate! For I tell you that you will never see me again until you say, 'Blessed be He who comes in the name of the Lord.'"*

Al was quick to remark, "When you showed us the genealogy, at the beginning, I used the 'mild Australian expletive' as Stephen termed it. It is time to say again. 'Strewth' and to wonder what Matthew was thinking of." But there were some other comments. Andrew remarked that the injunction to follow the teaching of the Pharisees but not their example seemed a bit odd. He wondered if this came from an early stage in the teaching of Jesus. Then Webster had a word or three about phylacteries which, he said, are now better known as "tefillim" and he explained, unnecessarily, what they were. Melanie contributed a remark about the instruction "to call no man Father," thinking of the way that Anglicans and Roman Catholics addressed their clergy. "Jeremias remarks that the title 'Abba' is to be guarded" She also recalled an incident from her childhood when someone came to her house asking if "Father Jenkins" was available. She, being rather jealous for her father's attention, said, "He's not your father, he's my Father," and closed the door. And so it went on, with one commenting on the obsessive commitment to tithing and purity of household items, another about the death of Zechariah.

But then Martha had something more substantive to offer. " I have thought that there is a similarity between these verses and the Beatitudes of Chapter 4. They are almost mirror images," she said. "I have an article about the fundamental values in society at that time, of honor and shame, with the suggestion being that one can think of the Beatitudes as an honor code: 'Worthy are the poor for theirs is the Kingdom' and so on, and these verses in chapter 23 could be written, 'Shame on you Pharisees . . . ' Evidently, honor and shame were dominant categories in that world." This gave rise to a conversation which included references to the continuing place of "honor" in large parts of the world and to the distressing accounts of "honor" killings, especially of women. Andrew remarked that one could view crucifixion in this context, as the most shameful thing that could be envisioned; that early Christians could "glory in the cross of Christ" as St. Paul puts it, is an extraordinary thing. "If Jesus, by his life and words, came to turn society on its ear, the crucifixion and its subsequent part in the Christian proclamation, turns the most fundamental categories up-side-down!" Al continued this conversation with a remark that the growth of Christianity to become the dominant religion in the Mediterranean world is so surprising. Webster continued this thought by remarking, "The preaching was not so much the cross as the resurrection, the sign that the one who had been shamed in death, had been raised to new life in honor."

But there was one more piece to be considered: Martha drew their attention to the last section, Jesus lamenting over Jerusalem. She pointed out the feminine imagery: Jesus as the mother wishing to gather "her" children into safety. "But what about the last sentence," she asked. "Here is Jesus saying that Jerusalem won't see him again until he comes in triumph. Yet he is about to enter the city for his final ordeal." Webster reminded them that the order in which Matthew presented his material is not necessarily the chronological order. "Maybe Jesus said this before the Palm Sunday entrance." But Al objected that Matthew, for all his faults, wasn't likely to mess up the order to this extent. There the matter rested, another mystery!

It was time to go, and Melanie dismissed them with considerable relief that the chapter had generated some good discussion.

Chapter 24

Later that same week, Al and Melanie were back in the coffee shop, deep in conversation. She had realized early on that Al needed a confidant and, although she was uneasy in that role, she could scarcely avoid it.

He wanted to tell her of his experiences in Australia. "I hope you don't mind me going on a bit, about my early days but I realize that my upbringing still influences me too much. I think that I told you that I was brought up by my mother and that she bore great anger towards my father and towards the church. So I wasn't baptized and I was fed a steady diet of hostility to any form of religious belief or practice." He paused to savor his latte and wiped his mouth on the napkin before continuing. "But there was something else going on. My mother had a succession of men passing through her life; usually moving into the house but these relationships always ended up with great anger and hostility. When I was going through my father's papers, I came across many of the letters she had written to him after they had separated and one could deduce from what she wrote, that he had been trying to be reconciled but that she always rejected him. I guess that for the first time, I began to see the situation from his point of view after all those years of being told how he had abused her."

As he paused, Melanie wondered how to respond. What was he needing from her? Maybe just someone who would listen. But he wasn't finished. "My parting with my mother last week had some feeling of finality. I tried to tell her of my painful memories of childhood but she pushed me away and told me to grow up. So my trip to Australia has these two events which remain in my mind: taking communion at the cathedral and cutting the apron strings with my mother."

She needed to push the conversation away from the mother-son conflict and remarked, "It was interesting that you chose to share with the group on Tuesday your experience of taking communion. Al, where is all of this leading? Are you looking for a church, maybe committed to the 'radical inclusiveness' idea?" He looked pensive. "I am thinking that our group gives me a taste for community and if I could find something like that maybe you would see me in the pew."

"Or maybe, I would hear about it," she replied. "I am not as far along that road as you seem to think. But size is something to consider. Cathedrals and large parishes can be impersonal and that's what some people are looking for. Our group is a little community but churches of that size are usually in the process of dying."

"Perhaps we need to start our own church," he suggested, "with limited membership. Twelve sounds about right. No paid clergy, we couldn't afford them. Did you ever read Haldane's article, 'On being the right size'? He was a great biologist thinking about sizes of animals and so on but I wonder what is the right size for a church community." They pondered this question for a few moments but, receiving no inspiration about a reasonable answer, they decided to finish their coffee and depart.

Melanie had been apprehensive about Chapter 23 and had somewhat similar feelings about Chapter 24, the so-called Matthean Apocalypse. She knew that predictions of the end of the world were part of Holy Writ and she also knew how much time and effort had gone into many interpretations of the same texts. A little time looking into commentaries revealed that the situation was even more complicated: was Jesus predicting the end of the world or only the imminent destruction of Jerusalem? And, in either case, were these the product of the early church rather than words of Jesus himself?

So again when they gathered, Melanie was unable to give much by way of introduction. She resorted to her strategy, used before, of confessing ignorance and hoping that others would be better informed. The first little piece was not so troublesome:

> *Jesus had left the Temple and was going on his way, when his disciples came and called his attention to the Temple buildings. "You see all these?" he replied; "in solemn truth I tell you that there will not be left here one stone upon another that will not be pulled down."*

They had all read about the destruction of Jerusalem and its temple in the year 70. There seemed little to say except to recognize that this was an overwhelming disaster for the Jewish people. Andrew had read of proposals for rebuilding the Temple. "A bit tricky since the Mosque of Omar occupies the site. But the idea is supported by Christian fundamentalists who believe it must be there for the Second Coming and some ultra-orthodox Jews who need it for the Messiah to come. It reminds me of Teddy Kollek who was Mayor of Jerusalem. He was reputed to have said, 'When the Messiah comes, I will ask him if it is his first visit to Jerusalem.'"

Now Melanie was able to introduce the beginning of the mysterious discourse about the last days:

> *Afterwards he was on the Mount of Olives and was seated there when the disciples came to him, apart from the others, and said, "Tell us when this will be; and what will be the sign of your coming and of the Close of the Age?"*
>
> *"Take care that no one misleads you," answered Jesus "for many will come assuming my name and saying 'I am the Christ;' and they will mislead many.*
>
> *And, before long, you will hear of wars and rumors of wars. Do not be alarmed, for such things must be; but the End is not yet. For nation will rise in arms against nation, kingdom against kingdom, and there will be famines and earthquakes in various places; but all these miseries are but like the early pains of childbirth.*
>
> *At that time they will deliver you up to punishment and will put you to death; and you will be objects of hatred to all the nations because you are called by my name. Then will many stumble and fall, and they will betray one another and hate one another. Many false prophets will rise up and lead multitudes astray; and because of the prevalent disregard of God's law, the love of the great majority will grow cold; but those who stand firm to the End shall be saved. And this Good News of the Kingdom shall be proclaimed throughout the whole world to set the evidence before all the Gentiles; and then the End will come."*

They had been doing their homework and Stephen was quick to ask what the disciples could have meant by asking for "the sign of your coming," as though they had already been made aware of "his departure." He wondered why Matthew threw this at the reader without warning. "I know that we can't take his order of presentation as the chronological order but Jesus has given only the prediction thus far that he would be crucified and would return to life. Surely this must be a creation of the early church for whom the awaited 'coming' was a preoccupation." Andrew recalled that the early church had "prophets" who would give inspired utterances. "Possibly some of these prophets would speak in such a way that their words would be understood as a continuation of the words of Jesus. So it wouldn't be surprising if some of their words became part of the Gospel." Martha was enthusiastic about this idea. "It gets us past the notion that there was any fraud in the process!" Looking ahead, Stephen backed this up with the observation that the text envisions a world-wide proclamation before the End. "It's easy to hear this from the early church but it would be strange from the lips of Jesus before his death." Not everyone agreed with this; there was a feeling that "strange" was a reasonable description of most of the teaching of Jesus! Al was able look ahead even further. "If we are to think about the contribution of the early church, prophets or what-have-you, we will need also to look at the prediction further on, that 'this generation will not pass away until all these things come true.' We struggled with this question a few weeks ago." Melanie reminded them that it had been quite a few weeks ago. "This was in Chapter 10, I think, when Jesus sends out the disciples on their missionary journey and says that they wouldn't have finished it before the Son of Man comes. From what I have read, this question is fiercely debated, of whether Jesus made predictions which didn't come true, or whether the early church, within that 'generation', might have tried to encouraged its missionary outreach by including such predictions." Webster had one other comment. "There have been attempts," he said, "to show that the word 'genea', which is usually translated 'generation', can also mean 'race'. But the scholars seem unconvinced. Of course, we do not know what Jesus might have said in Aramaic so the matter remains a bit of a mystery. Most people are hesitant to come right out and say that Jesus was just mistaken! If he was mistaken in this, then we might begin to wonder about many other things he taught."

The ensuing conversation made it clear that they all found this totally confusing. And it didn't get easier as they confronted:

When you have seen (to use the language of the Prophet Daniel) the "Abomination of Desolation," standing in the Holy Place-(let the reader observe those words)- then let those who are in Judea escape to the hills; let him who is on the roof not go down to fetch what is in his house; nor let him who is outside the city stay to pick up his outer garment. And alas for the women who at that

> *time are with child or have infants! But pray that your flight may not be in winter, nor on the Sabbath; for it will be a time of great suffering, such as never has been from the beginning of the world till now, and assuredly never will be again. And if those days had not been cut short, no one would escape; but for the sake of God's own people those days will be cut short.*

More problems! At least, they all knew that the "Abomination of Desolation" was a reference to the desecration of the Temple by the Greek invaders about a century and a half before the time of Jesus. Stephen said, "It could be argued that all of this section refers to the destruction of Jerusalem and its temple in AD 70. But I am puzzled about the reference to the Sabbath. Surely those fleeing for their lives would not be not be constrained by the restriction on travel on the Sabbath?" Webster wondered if the problem would be that the refugees would not be able to obtain supplies for their journey if they set out on a Sabbath Day. "But in what ways were the days cut short, presumably the number of days rather than the days themselves; the siege of Jerusalem was, in fact, a drawn out affair of more than six months. And when the Temple was destroyed, its Holy Place was destroyed and so where did the 'abomination of desolation' stand?"

There was a general feeling of helplessness and, for once, Melanie thought that it would be pleasant to have an "expert" to explain it all. But she realized that the "experts" did not agree among themselves so it was not such a great idea. And there was more:

> *If at that time any one should say to you, "See, here is the Christ!" or "Here!", give no credence to it. For there will rise up false Christs and false prophets, displaying wonderful signs and prodigies, so as to deceive, were it possible, even God's own people. Remember, I have forewarned you.*
>
> *If therefore they should say to you, "See, He is in the desert!," do not go out there: or "See, He is indoors in the room!," do not believe it.*
>
> *For just as the lightning flashes in the east and is seen to the very west, so will be the coming of the Son of Man. Wherever the dead body is, there will the vultures flock together.*
>
> *But immediately after those times of distress, the sun will be darkened, the moon will not shed her light, the stars will fall from the firmament, and the forces which control the heavens will be*

disordered and disturbed. Then will appear the sign of the Son of Man in the sky; and then will all the nations of the earth lament, when they see the Son of Man coming on the clouds of the sky with great power and glory. And He will send out His angels with a loud trumpet-blast, and they will bring together His own people to Him from north, south, east and west—from one extremity of the world to the other.

Al expressed the sense that the group was growing weary of all this. "There have always been Christians who get fascinated with this kind of thing and try to map out the future. Maybe we should leave them to get on with it and we should get on with Matthew!" Stephen had the last word by quoting Mark Twain: "It ain't the parts of the Bible that I can't understand that bother me, it's the parts that I do understand."

So Melanie presented them with the last section all together:

"Now learn from the fig-tree the lesson it teaches. As soon as its branches have now become soft and it is bursting into leaf, you all know that summer is near. So you also, when you see all these signs, may be sure that he is near—at your very door.

I tell you in solemn truth that the present generation will certainly not pass away without all these things having first taken place. Earth and sky will pass away, but it is certain that my words will not pass away.

But as to that day and the exact time no one knows—not even the angels of heaven, nor the Son, but the Father alone. For as it was in the time of Noah, so it will be at the coming of the Son of Man. At that time, before the Deluge, men were busy eating and drinking, taking wives or giving them, up to the very day when Noah entered the Ark, nor did they realise any danger till the Deluge came and swept them all away; so will it be at the coming of the Son of Man.

Then will two men be in the open country: one will be taken away, and one left behind. Two women will be grinding at the mill: one will be taken away, and one left behind. Be on the alert therefore, for you do not know the day on which your Lord is coming.

But of this be assured, that if the master of the house had known the hour at which the robber was coming, he would have kept awake, and not have allowed his house to be broken into. Therefore you also must be ready; for it is at a time when you do not expect Him that the Son of Man will come.

Who therefore is the loyal and intelligent servant to whom his master has entrusted the control of his household to give them their rations at the appointed time? Blessed is that servant whom his master when he comes shall find so doing! In solemn truth I tell you that he will give him the management of all his wealth. But if the man, being a bad servant, should say in his heart, 'My master is a long time in coming,' and should begin to beat his fellow servants, while he eats and drinks with drunkards; the master of that servant will arrive on a day when he is not expecting him and at an hour of which he has not been informed; he will treat him with the utmost severity and assign him a place among the hypocrites: there will be the weeping and the gnashing of teeth."

There was a silence in the room and a reluctance to discuss this at all. For the first time, she sensed rebellion! It was time to go!

Chapter 25

MELANIE HADN'T KNOWN THAT Al lived "over the store". He had invited her to come around for drinks on Friday evening, to meet "someone you might find interesting". So at 5 p.m., she made her way through the bookstore and up the back stairs to discover that he lived in some comfort in his bachelor apartment: a large room, filled with books, "overflow from down below," he explained, with kitchen at one end and bedroom at the other. Outlook through large windows, overlooking the park. Not such a bad inheritance, she thought.

The person to meet was someone she had been somewhat aware of, Alison Thomasson. Known as Ally to her friends, she was the chaplain at a large retirement community, St. George's House, nearby. After some preliminaries, Al making sure that drinks and nibbles were within reach, he explained what he had in mind. He gave Ally some indication of his recent thinking about church and Christian belief, based on the Matthew group, his visit to Australia and his conversations with Melanie. "I have heard about your chapel community," he said, addressing Ally, " and wondered if it might be a place where someone like me might find a home." She replied that she wasn't sure what he was looking for, but that certainly the Sunday chapel service with a simple celebration of Holy Communion and some "fair to middling music," did attract a number of people from outside St George's. "Some of them come to help us bring the less mobile residents to the service but there are some others who are simply there, for various reasons. I am glad they come and don't really want to know why they come to our chapel rather than a regular church service." Melanie could see why Al might find Ally's gentle openness encouraging. Their conversation drifted away to other things, but eventually they separated with Alison's invitation, "Just come along and check us out."

Al was keen to follow that up and equally keen that Melanie should accompany him. But she explained that she was away visiting her father that coming Sunday; later she realized that she was finding Al's intensity a bit much. "He's almost like a new convert," she thought, although she hadn't had much contact with "new converts" of any stripe.

The weekend was taken up with some reading of Matthew 25, making her realize that some of the discussions of the previous two weeks were likely to reoccur, and then the visit to her father, who now didn't recognize her. She came back feeling depressed by her long journey and the memory of her father's state.

By Monday, she was back at the coffee shop at Al's invitation. He was eager to share his experience of the previous day. She rather wished that he might think to ask after her father's wellbeing but he was preoccupied with the chapel service. "Maybe," he said, "this is the way forward. Ally has a nice touch. She preached a small homily and had some sensible things to say about hope as a guide to life. And she was understated about the music. There is a nicely voiced pipe organ and the organist knows his stuff. By the way, she is known as RevAlly at St George's and seems to have something special going on." Melanie was impressed but not surprised. Aunt Matty sometimes used the expression "all his geese are swans" and she recognized the signs of an enthusiast. "I'm glad that you have not been disappointed," she said. "So do you think this is where you will be found on Sunday mornings?" He was thoughtful about that possibility and expressed an opinion that it would not be enough to simply sit in the pew. "Maybe I will volunteer to do some visiting." She wondered how long his enthusiasm would last.

Back home, she turned her attention again to the coming chapter. At least, it had some parables to look at; and the Last Judgement scene would keep them busy. So as they gathered again, she was confident that they would have a good evening together. Firstly, they tackled the Bridesmaids parable:

> *Then will the Kingdom of Heaven be found to be like ten bridesmaids who took their torches and went out to meet the bridegroom. Five of them were foolish and five were wise. For the foolish, when they took their torches, did not provide themselves with oil; but the wise, besides their torches, took oil in their flasks. The bridegroom was a long time in coming, so that meanwhile they all became drowsy and fell asleep.*
>
> *But at midnight there is a loud cry, "The bridegroom! Go out and meet him!" Then all those bridesmaids roused themselves and trimmed their torches.*

"Give us some of your oil," said the foolish ones to the wise, "for our torches are going out."

"But perhaps," replied the wise, "there will not be enough for all of us. Go to the shops rather, and buy some for yourselves."

So they went to buy. But meanwhile the bridegroom came; those bridesmaids who were ready went in with him to the wedding banquet; and the door was shut. Afterwards the other bridesmaids came and cried, "Sir, Sir, open the door to us."

"In solemn truth I tell you," he replied, "I do not know you." Keep awake therefore; for you know neither the day nor the hour.

They avoided the debate about the origin of this parable. "If Jesus taught it," said Al, "it would be a bit mysterious to the disciples." And no one wanted to pursue this. But they agreed that being alert for the coming of the Kingdom was a new emphasis although urgency had been implicit in some parts of the earlier teaching. Webster recalled, from Chapter 8, the man who wished to follow Jesus and was forbidden even to bury his father. Also the sense of the missionary tour of Chapter 10 of travelling light and not staying around to debate with anyone who showed a lack of welcome. And the second parable along the same lines.

> *Why, it is like a man who, when going on his travels, called his bondservants and entrusted his property to their care. To one he gave five talents, to another two, to another one— to each according to his individual capacity; and then started from home. Without delay the one who had received the five talents went and employed them in business, and gained five more.*
>
> *In the same way he who had the two gained two more. But the man who had received the one went and dug a hole and buried his master's money.*
>
> *After a long lapse of time the master of those servants returned, and had a reckoning with them. The one who had received the five talents came and brought five more, and said, "Sir, it was five talents that you entrusted to me: see, I have gained five more."*
>
> *"You have done well, good and trustworthy servant," replied his master; "you have been trustworthy in the management of a little, I will put you in charge of much: share your master's joy."*
>
> *The second, who had received the two talents, came and said, "Sir, it was two talents you entrusted to me: see, I have gained two more."*

> "Good and trustworthy servant, you have done well," his master replied; "you have been trustworthy in the management of a little, I will put you in charge of much: share your master's joy."
>
> But, next, the man who had the one talent in his keeping came and said, "Sir, I knew you to be a severe man, reaping where you had not sown and garnering what you had not winnowed. So being afraid, I went and buried your talent in the ground: there you have what belongs to you."
>
> "You wicked and slothful servant," replied his master, "did you know that I reap where I have not sown, and garner what I have not winnowed? Your duty then was to deposit my money in some bank, and so when I came I should have got back my property with interest. So take away the talent from him, and give it to the man who has the ten."
>
> (For to every one who has, more shall be given, and he shall have abundance; but from him who has nothing, even what he has shall be taken away.)
>
> "But as for this worthless servant, put him out into the darkness outside: there will be the weeping and the gnashing of teeth."

Stephen remarked upon the coincidence that the word "talent" meant something different to us, not a unit of currency any more. "It is almost irresistible for preachers to use that coincidence and urge us not to squander natural abilities. But the original seems to mean something quite different." Melanie was not entirely surprised that there was little energy to discuss these parables. She supposed that it was because the Last Judgement section was uppermost in their minds and so she moved on:

> When the Son of Man comes in His glory, and all the angels with Him, then will He sit upon His glorious throne, and all the nations will be gathered into His presence. And He will separate them from one another, just as a shepherd separates the sheep from the goats; and will make the sheep stand at His right hand, and the goats at His left.
>
> Then the King will say to those at His right, "Come, my Father's blessed ones, receive your inheritance of the Kingdom which has been divinely intended for you ever since the creation of the world. For when I was hungry, you gave me food; when I was thirsty, you gave me drink; when I was homeless, you gave me a welcome;

when I was ill-clad, you clothed me; when I was sick, you visited me; when I was in prison, you came to see me."

"When, Lord," the righteous will reply, "did we see you hungry and feed you; or thirsty, and give you drink? When did we see you homeless, and give you a welcome? or ill-clad, and clothe you? When did we see you sick or in prison, and come to see you?"

But the King will answer them, "In solemn truth I tell you that in so far as you rendered such services to one of the humblest of these my brethren, you rendered them to myself."

Then will He say to those at His left, "Begone from me, with the curse resting upon you, into the eternal fire, which has been prepared for the Devil and his angels. For when I was hungry, you gave me nothing to eat; when thirsty, you gave me nothing to drink; when homeless, you gave me no welcome; ill-clad, you clothed me not; sick or in prison, you visited me not."

Then will they also answer, "Lord, when did we see Thee hungry or thirsty or homeless or ill-clad or sick or in prison, and not come to serve Thee?"

But he will reply, "In solemn truth I tell you that in so far as you withheld such services from one of the humblest of these, you withheld them from me."

And these shall go away into eternal punishment, but the righteous into eternal life.

"This is certainly one of the most famous passages in Matthew's Gospel," she remarked, "and has no parallels in the other gospels." Webster wanted his say. "It has been problematic to Protestants who follow Paul's teachings about justification by faith. It seems that good works can get you into heaven after all." Martha recalled her Catholic education. "We were taught that 'faith' means more than intellectual assent. Maybe 'salvation by faith alone' should be replaced by 'salvation by being faithful to Christ.'"

Webster wasn't finished. "There has been an ongoing debate over the identity of 'the humblest of these, my brethren'. When I did a Google search on the matter, I came across a reference of a book by Sherman Gray devoted to this Last Judgement passage. It is a good reminder to me that so much can be said on the topic. In particular, would you believe that he identifies no less than thirty two interpretations of the 'humblest of these, my brethren'!" There was some relief that Webster wasn't going to give details but he did go on to give his opinion that identifying them with the world's poor cannot be the primary meaning. "It seems clear that 'my brethren' are the persecuted disciples and the nations are being judged by their treatment of them." This caused quite a lively discussion. Al wanted to know if that gets us off the hook as far as charity to the poor is concerned. "Maybe I won't have to feel so guilty when I pass by a panhandler without responding!" he suggested. But it was pointed out that care for the poor was enjoined in many other parts of Scripture so he wasn't free from that. Stephen wondered if collective judgement was envisioned. "Would the Chinese be judged by their treatment of Christian minorities?" Again, a lively discussion of the destiny of nations that had no Christian minorities; lively, imaginative but with no consensus reached.

How often they had ended their sessions with minds filled with unanswered questions (or perhaps "unanswerable questions"). They had grown accustomed to this and again, as they left, somehow seemed content.

Chapter 26

Early on, Melanie had looked at her calendar and observed that they would finish their journey through Matthew's gospel in the week after Easter. This coincidence, that they would be reading the story of the death of Jesus during Holy Week and the Resurrection narrative two days after Easter Sunday, seemed a bit uncanny. As if that was not enough, the Cathedral Choir with orchestra and soloists would present the St Matthew's Passion during Holy Week. She had some kind of impression that she was being pushed from all sides and she thought she could, again, hear Aunt Matty's chuckles. But she was not going to give in so easily! Al could do what he liked and become a card carrying Christian with bells and whistles, if that was his choice. She began reading Hitchens, "God is Not Good," but soon gave it up, appalled by such angry polemic.

As was now her usual practice, she set herself to read the text before Tuesday came, knowing that the next two sessions would cover the events referred to as "The Passion." She didn't expect any surprises. It was all well known stuff: Jesus, betrayed by Judas, deserted by the other disciples, is subjected to a trial, condemned on trumped up evidence, and goes to his death. She didn't anticipate the emotional reaction to the reading. It wasn't so familiar, after all. But more than that, she realized how horrifying it all was and in some way, she felt the pain of human suffering, deep within herself. By Tuesday, she felt an unaccustomed restlessness of spirit and she hoped that it wouldn't show. It wouldn't do, at all, to be distracted by inner turmoil.

But when they began, she decided to share some of this with the group. "There is something here," she admitted, "which is deeply disturbing." Not all of them responded and she supposed that constant familiarity with the text might blunt its impact for some of them. So they began:

> *When Jesus had ended all these discourses, he said to his disciples, "You know that in two days' time the Passover comes. And the Son of Man will be delivered up to be crucified."*
>
> *Then the High Priests and elders of the people assembled in the court of the palace of the High Priest Caiaphas, and consulted how to get Jesus into their power by stratagem and put him to death. But they said, "Not during the Festival, lest there be a riot among the people."*

Webster needed his say. "We all know about the Passover so I'm not going to talk about that. But I have been surprised to read through to the end and to discover that the Pharisees seem to disappear from view. Are they included among the 'elders of the people', I wonder?" Another question which needed to be left unsettled as they proceeded to the anointing narrative.

> *Now when Jesus was come to Bethany and was at the house of Simon the Leper, a woman came to him with a jar of very costly, sweet-scented ointment, which she poured over his head as he reclined at table. "Why such waste?" indignantly exclaimed the disciples; "for this might have been sold for a considerable sum, and the money given to the poor."*
>
> *But Jesus heard it, and said to them, "Why are you vexing her? For she has done a most gracious act towards me. The poor you always have with you, but me you have not always. In pouring this ointment over me, her object was to prepare me for burial. In solemn truth I tell you that wherever in the whole world this Good News shall be proclaimed, this deed of hers shall be spoken of in memory of her."*

Not surprisingly, Martha was eager to speak and she spoke with great passion. "There is something extraordinarily touching about this story. If we ignore the churlishness of the disciples, we can hear Jesus in his most tender mood. The last part is particularly important, I think. This unnamed woman and her act of compassion is celebrated as no other. Who else in the Gospels wins such an accolade?"

Webster could not allow Martha her special moment. "Not quite an unnamed woman, I believe. John's Gospel identifies her as Mary of Bethany." Melanie realized that, in spite of their years of friendship, she was growing ever more impatient with Webster. She was grateful when Martha replied, "Why are you vexing me? Know you not that Mary of Bethany is recorded as having anointed the feet of Jesus not his head!" Webster had the grace to look abashed.

She went on to recall the symbolism of anointing of kings and priests, and of the newly dead, of the Magi who included myrrh among their gifts and the account in John's Gospel of the embalming of the body of Jesus by Nicodemus and Joseph of Arimathea. There was a lot to think about.

After a pause, Stephen surprised them all by thanking Martha for her contribution. He went on to comment on the remark Jesus made about 'the poor being always with you' as an example of a statement being made in context to the disciples: "Go ahead, if you are so concerned about the poor. There are plenty of them around and there will be endless opportunities for you to help them. But this is a 'magic moment'. Don't spoil it."

Melanie was impressed by the gentleness of his rebuke to Webster and hoped that it would do some good. But it was important to move along as there was so much more to cover:

> At that time one of the Twelve, the one called Judas Iscariot, went to the High Priests and said, "What are you willing to give me if I betray him to you?" So they weighed out to him thirty shekels, and from that moment he was on the look out for an opportunity to betray him.

The contrast between the anointing story and this dismal episode scarcely needed to be stressed. Andrew had taken the trouble to discover that the "shekel" was worth about four day's pay for a laborer so that thirty shekels constituted a sizable bribe. "At least the equivalent of several thousand dollars in modern currency, if my information is correct."

But there was a feeling that the narrative of the Last Supper was urgently needing their consideration:

> On the first day of the Unleavened Bread the disciples came to Jesus with the question, "Where shall we make preparations for you to eat the Passover?"
>
> "Go into the city," he replied, "to a certain man, and tell him, 'The Teacher says, My time is close at hand. It is at your house

> that I shall keep the Passover with my disciples'." The disciples did as Jesus directed them, and got the Passover ready.
>
> When evening came, he was at table with the twelve disciples, and the meal was proceeding, when Jesus said, "In solemn truth I tell you that one of you will betray me." Intensely grieved, they began one after another to ask him, "Can it be I, Master?"
>
> "The one who has dipped his fingers in the bowl with me," he answered, "is the man who will betray me. The Son of Man is indeed going as is written concerning him; but alas for that man by whom the Son of Man is betrayed! It had been a happy thing for that man if he had never been born."
>
> Then Judas, the disciple who was betraying him, asked, "Can it be I, Rabbi?"
>
> "It is you," he replied.

Webster, having now recovered his equilibrium, wondered why the final sentence was included. "Mark and Luke leave the identity of the betrayer uncertain. And John identifies Judas as the betrayer but in such a way that the disciples seem not to understand." Melanie wasn't sure if this line of thought was fruitful and since no one wanted to comment, she moved on to the institution of the Eucharist.

> During the meal Jesus took a Passover bread, blessed it and broke it. He then gave it to the disciples, saying, "Take this and eat it: it is my body." And he took the cup and gave thanks, and gave it to them saying, "Drink from it, all of you, for this is my blood which is to be poured out for many for the remission of sins—the blood which ratifies the Covenant. I tell you that I will never again take the produce of the vine till that day when I shall drink the new wine with you in my Father's Kingdom."
>
> So they sang the hymn and went out to the Mount of Olives.

Melanie began by observing that no text in the New Testament had received more scrutiny than this. "And none has created more controversy. Those few words, 'It is my body', have divided Christendom!" Stephen said that it all seemed to depend on whether Jesus was speaking metaphorically or not. "As Bill Clinton said, it depends on what the meaning of the word 'is' is." There was some shock but mainly uncomprehending silence around the table. "As I recall it," said Webster, "Clinton was trying to justify his previous denials relating to sexual misbehavior. I'm sorry that you reminded us of that. Especially in this context!" Stephen had the grace to look suitably cowed by this rebuke.

They were relieved when Andrew remarked that from this passage on its own, repetition of the event might not have been expected. "But evidently, it was the practice of the early church to make it the central part of worship." There was some general discussion about experience of the Eucharist. Al spoke of the chapel service at the hospital without revealing much about his own participation. Stephen, sensing that he had offended some, tried to make amends: "Before forks and spoons, bread passed around gave opportunity for each to break off a piece to use to scoop up food from the common dish. And the common cup was a universal sign of inclusion and fellowship." He wondered what the disciples thought about it. "The idea of eating flesh and drinking blood would have been totally shocking." Webster wanted to contest this point, using John's Gospel. "After the feeding story in John 6, Jesus gives the long discussion of the 'bread which came down from heaven.' He says that he is the true bread and must be eaten in order to obtain eternal life. If this has some historical basis, then maybe the disciples weren't entirely taken by surprise at the Last Supper."

Melanie thought that they might leave the matter, expressing frustration that so much was again left unsettled. So they looked at:

> Then said Jesus, "This night all of you will stumble and fail in your fidelity to me; for it is written, 'I will strike the Shepherd, and the sheep of the flock will be scattered in all directions.' But after I have risen to life again, I will go before you into Galilee."
>
> "All may stumble and fail," said Peter, "but I never will."
>
> "In solemn truth I tell you," replied Jesus, "that this very night, before the cock crows, you will three times disown me."
>
> "Even if I must die with you," declared Peter, "I will never disown you." In like manner protested all the disciples.

Al came up with the interesting observation about the skilful interweaving of light and darkness. "It goes back and forth, first a prediction of crucifixion and conspiracy among the enemies of Jesus. Then the anointing at Bethany; next Judas and his offer to betray, finally the Last Supper with its own contrast between the prediction of the failure of the disciples, and the institution of the Eucharist. Now another prediction of the disciples' failure followed, in a bit, by the Gethsemane episode and the final arrest. Sometimes Matthew, the writer, had a good day!"

But apart from reflections on style, they wished to speak of failure, some painful memories emerging from the group. "I guess," remarked Melanie, "we all carry memories of brave resolutions not carried out in practice." There was another pause. It seemed that they all had private memories over which to linger.

After a while, Melanie moved them along:

> *Then Jesus came with them to a place called Gethsemane. And he said to the disciples, "Sit down here, whilst I go yonder and there pray. And he took with him Peter and the two sons of Zebedee. Then he began to be full of anguish and distress, and he said to them, "My soul is crushed with anguish to the very point of death; wait here, and keep awake with me." Going forward a short distance he fell on his face and prayed. "My Father," he said, "if it is possible, let this cup pass away from me; nevertheless, not as I will, but as Thou willest." Then he came to the disciples and found them asleep, and he said to Peter, "Alas, none of you could keep awake with me for even a single hour! Keep awake, and pray that you may not enter into temptation: the spirit is right willing, but the body is frail." Again a second time he went away and prayed, saying, "My Father, if it is impossible for this cup to pass without my drinking it, Thy will be done." He came and again found them asleep, for they were very tired. So he left them, and went away once more and prayed a third time, again using the same words.*
>
> *Then he came to the disciples and said, "Sleep on and rest. See, the moment is close at hand when the Son of Man is to be betrayed into the hands of sinful men. Rouse yourselves. Let us be going. My betrayer is close at hand."*

Al wondered how anyone would know of this private struggle if indeed the disciples were asleep. Looking more carefully at the text, Andrew drew their attention to the rather confusing description of the "disciples." "There seems to be once again the choice of Peter, James and John who accompany Jesus, leaving the others behind. He describes his anguish to the three and then goes forward 'a short distance'. When he returns, he finds 'the disciples' asleep but then speaks to Peter who is evidently awake. Perhaps 'the disciples' in this case refers to the remaining eight. It would be eight since we soon learn that Judas has slipped away."

Martha remarked how real the temptation might have been since there would have been ample opportunity to escape in the darkness. Now the pace quickens:

> *He had scarcely finished speaking when Judas came—one of the Twelve—accompanied by a great crowd of men armed with swords and bludgeons, sent by the High Priests and Elders of the People.*
>
> *Now the betrayer had agreed upon a sign with them, to direct them. He had said, "The one whom I kiss is the man: lay hold of him." So he went straight to Jesus and said, "Peace to you, Rabbi!" And he kissed him eagerly. "Friend," said Jesus, "carry out your intention." Then they came and laid their hands on Jesus and seized him firmly. But one of those with Jesus drew his sword and struck the High Priest's servant, cutting off his ear. "Put back your sword again," said Jesus, "for all who draw the sword shall perish by the sword. Or do you suppose I cannot entreat my Father and He would instantly send to my help more than twelve legions of angels? In that case how are the Scriptures to be fulfilled which declare that thus it must be?"*
>
> *Then said Jesus to the crowds, "Have you come out as if to fight with a robber, with swords and bludgeons to apprehend me? Day after day I have been sitting teaching in the Temple, and you did not arrest me. But all this has taken place in order that the writings of the Prophets may be fulfilled." At this point the disciples all left him and fled.*

"Just in case we have forgotten, Judas is identified, 'one of the Twelve,'" observed Stephen. "It somehow heightens the horror of the moment and the traitor's kiss." Martha drew their attention to the adverb, "eagerly" to describe the kiss. " In some translations, it is 'tenderly'; what are we to make of this? It's too much! And Jesus addresses him ironically as 'friend'."

They thought about this. Melanie had this to say. "Maybe it's a reminder. However much we betray him, he still sees us as 'friend'. I'm not sure that I'm ready for that!"

Again it was Webster who couldn't hold back. "John's Gospel tells us that it was Peter who drew the sword, the High Priest's servant's name was Malchus and Jesus miraculously restored the severed ear." Melanie wished that Webster wouldn't feel this need to inform them; maybe his way of avoiding the personal.

> But the officers who had laid hold of Jesus led him away to Caiaphas the High Priest, at whose house the Scribes and the Elders had assembled. And Peter kept following him at a distance, till he came even to the court of the High Priest's palace, where he entered and sat down among the officers to see the issue. Meanwhile the High Priests and the whole Sanhedrin were seeking false testimony against Jesus in order to put him to death; but they could find none, although many false witnesses came forward. At length there came two who testified, "This man said, 'I am able to pull down the Sanctuary of God and three days afterwards to build a new one.'" Then the High Priest stood up and asked him, "Have you no answer to make? What is it these men are saying in evidence against you?"
>
> Jesus however remained silent. Again the High Priest addressed him. "In the name of the ever-living God," he said, "I now put you on your oath. Tell us whether you are the Christ, the Son of God."
>
> "I am He," replied Jesus. "But I tell you that, later on, you will see the Son of Man sitting at the right hand of power, and coming on the clouds of the sky." Then the High Priest tore his robes and exclaimed, "Impious language! What further need have we of witnesses! See, you have now heard the impiety. What is your verdict?"
>
> "He deserves to die," they replied. Then they spat in his face, and struck him—some with the fist, some with the open hand- while they taunted him, saying, "Christ, prove yourself a Prophet by telling us who it was that struck you."

Some of them had read the various theories concerning the legality of the proceedings which now began. "It seemed important to maintain a semblance of justice even though they had bribed Judas and now presumably false witnesses," said Stephen. "The commandment against bearing false witness seems scarcely an issue." Al noted that the disciples had fled but Peter at least stayed within watching distance. "Give him credit for that."

Andrew pointed out that the reply that Jesus gives to the question is variously translated. "It is literally, 'you say', which seems to leave it ambiguous. In any case, was it an offence to claim to be the Messiah? And was the reference to the 'Son of Man' so obviously a reference to Jesus himself?" There ensued a confused discussion which generated neither light nor heat. "Anyway," said Stephen, "it seems to have been enough to bring a death sentence."

Martha reflected on the abuse suffered by the captive Jesus. "Where does all the hatred come from? Is there something in religion which brings it out?" Melanie thought about Hitchen's book and his affirmative answer to all such questions. The discussion went back and forth as they considered the mixed record of all religions: much evil and much good coming apparently from the same source. Martha spoke of hostility towards women in the church and Al reminded them of hatred towards gay people. They found it a sobering discussion. And there was now no let up as they considered personal failure:

> *Peter meanwhile was sitting outside in the court of the palace, when one of the maidservants came over to him and said, "You too were with Jesus the Galilean." He denied it before them all, saying, "I do not know what you mean." Soon afterwards he went out and stood in the gateway, when another girl saw him, and said, addressing the people there, "This man was with Jesus the Nazarene." Again he denied it with an oath. "I do not know the man," he said. A short time afterwards the people standing there came and said to Peter, "Certainly you too are one of them, for your accent shows it." Then with curses and oaths he declared, "I do not know the man." Immediately a cock crowed, and Peter recollected the words of Jesus, how he had said, "Before the cock crows you will three times disown me." And he went out and wept aloud, bitterly.*

It had been a long evening and they scarcely had time or energy to face Peter's failure. They separated with the words, '. . . he went out and wept bitterly,' echoing in their minds and hearts.

Chapter 27

It was now Holy Week and Melanie thought of Holy Weeks long past when she had been taken along to church almost every evening as befitted the daughter of the Rector. How she had come to dread those long and melancholy hours. Being a Preacher's Kid wasn't all fun!

Al had emailed, giving his latest enthusiastic response to Sunday at the hospital chapel. Would she like to come with him on Easter Day? There would be baptisms, he said. Balloons and fireworks,too, for all she knew. She delayed a reply, aware that she was being a bit irrational in her response to what was happening. Why should Al's enthusiasm alienate her?

The text for the next Tuesday was in her mind. She had found information about crucifixion which only heightened the horror, that it combined the maximum of pain with an excess of humiliation. Most scholars seemed to agree that victims were naked on the cross; no modest draping of the genitals in that barbaric act. The Romans wanted to remind their captive peoples of the fate of those who rocked the boat. Depictions of crucifixion in art and sculpture generally avoided the nakedness of the crucified one. She found one exception: Michelangelo's crucifix in Santo Spirito, Florence, discreetly placed in a chapel. The aspect of humiliation lingered in her mind.

By Tuesday, she felt she was embarking on an ordeal, the journey through Chapter 27. They all seemed sober as they gathered and the conversation was muted. "Have you felt as I did?" she asked. "about to enter the heart of darkness?"

So they read:

> When morning came all the High Priests and the Elders of the people consulted together against Jesus to put Him to death; and binding him they led him away and handed him over to Pilate the Governor. Then when Judas, who had betrayed him, saw that he was condemned, smitten with remorse he brought back the thirty

> *shekels to the High Priests and Elders and said, "I have sinned, in betraying to death one who is innocent." "What does that matter to us?" they replied; "it is your business." Flinging the shekels into the Sanctuary, he left the place, and went and hanged himself.*
>
> *When the High Priests had gathered up the money they said, "It is illegal to put it into the Treasury, because it is the price of blood." So after consulting together they spent the money in the purchase of the Potter's Field as a burial place for people not belonging to the city; for which reason that piece of ground received the name, which it still bears, of "the Field of Blood."*
>
> *Then were fulfilled the words spoken by the Prophet Jeremiah, "And I took the thirty shekels, the price of the prized one on whom Israelites had set a price, and gave them for the potter's field, as the Lord directed me."*

They reflected on the fact that it was now the morning after the drama of the nighttime trial. No sleep for Jesus that night, nor for Peter in his despair. "Nor for Judas," added Stephen. "Do you remember someone mentioning Dorothy Sayers 'The Man Born to be King' when we discussed Chapter 10? The idea that Judas acted not as a traitor but as one who wished to force Jesus to act decisively to bring in the Kingdom? Well, the fact that he didn't show remorse until Jesus is condemned somehow supports that idea."

Webster needed to speak of the contradiction between this account of the action of Judas and that of the Acts of the Apostles where he himself buys a field and there "fell headlong, his body burst and his intestines spilled out." If Webster expected gratitude for such a detail, he was disappointed. Nor did they care for his explanation that the purported quote from Jeremiah was a composite of verses from Jeremiah and Zechariah. It seemed to Melanie that the group was showing their displeasure with Webster by ignoring him. They moved on:

> *Meanwhile Jesus was brought before the Governor, and the latter put the question, "Are you the King of the Jews?" "I am their King," he answered.*
>
> *When however the High Priests and the Elders kept bringing their charges against him, he said not a word in reply. "Do you not hear," asked Pilate, "what a mass of evidence they are bringing against you?" But he made no reply to a single accusation, so that the Governor was greatly astonished.*

Once again, Andrew mentioned that in the original, there is the seemingly ambiguous response to Pilate's question: "you say," which most translators interpret as an affirmative. "I am not knowledgeable about Greek but the translation that we are looking at seems rather strong. Perhaps in the original it meant something else . . ." His voice trailed off as he looked around for help but no one had any to offer.

> Now it was the Governor's custom at the Festival to release some one prisoner, whomsoever the populace desired; and at this time they had a notorious prisoner called Barabbas. So when they were now assembled Pilate appealed to them. "Whom shall I release to you," he said, "Barabbas, or Jesus the so-called Christ?" For he knew that it was from envious hatred that Jesus had been brought before him. While he was sitting on the tribunal a message came to him from his wife. "Have nothing to do with that innocent man," she said, "for during the night I have suffered terribly in a dream through him."
>
> The High Priests, however, and the Elders urged the crowd to ask for Barabbas and to demand the death of Jesus. So when the Governor a second time asked them, "Which of the two shall I release to you?"—they cried, "Barabbas!"
>
> "What then," said Pilate, "shall I do with Jesus, the so-called Christ?"
>
> With one voice they shouted, "Let him be crucified!"
>
> "Why, what crime has he committed?" asked Pilate. But they kept on furiously shouting, "Let him be crucified!" So when he saw that he could gain nothing, but that on the contrary there was a riot threatening, he called for water and washed his hands in sight of them all, saying, "I am not responsible for this murder : you must answer for it."
>
> "His blood," replied all the people, "be on us and on our children!"

Stephen knew that Barabbas, in some manuscripts, is called "Jesus Barabbas." "Maybe," he suggested, "an attempt to put the choice even more starkly. Which Jesus do you want?" They spent some moments considering Pilate's wife and her dream, and the famous hand-washing scene. Martha remarked that only Matthew, among the Gospel writers, mentions the episode of Pilate's wife and her dream; she wondered again whether this was the sort of detail which a woman might include.

Andrew thought of the echoes of dreams in the nativity stories and the washing of the disciples' feet. "Sometimes I wish I were a preacher," he said. "Good sermon material here."

Martha reminded them of the deadly consequences of Matthew's inclusion of the final verse, an excuse for anti-Semitism from that day until this. "If only," she lamented, "he had included the saying from Luke: 'Father, forgive them, for they know not what they do.'" No one needed to be reminded of the lethal history of anti-Semitism in Christian history but they were sobered by Martha's words. Al had a thought of a different kind. "There is some kind of irony here. 'Blood' can mean two things. Death, on the one hand, but also redemption. Maybe the words of the people unconsciously point to their ultimate inclusion in the Kingdom." On this hopeful note, Melanie moved them along:

> *Then he released Barabbas to them, but Jesus he ordered to be scourged, and gave him up to be crucified. Then the Governor's soldiers took Jesus into the Praetorium, and called together the whole battalion to make sport of him. Stripping off his garments, they put on him a general's short crimson cloak. They twisted a wreath of thorny twigs and put it on his head, and they put a scepter of cane in his right hand, and kneeling to him they shouted in mockery, "Long live the King of the Jews!"*
>
> *Then they spat upon him, and taking the cane they repeatedly struck him on the head with it. At last, having finished their sport, they took off the cloak, clothed him again in his own garments, and led him away for crucifixion.*

Stephen wished to remind them of Mel Gibson's *The Passion of the Christ* that had attracted so much attention when it was first released. "It claims to be faithful to the text but when it devotes ten minutes to the scourging, one can only wonder. Roger Ebert said it was the most violent film he had ever seen. The text suggests that scourging was a routine part of the punishment, horrible no doubt, but not something in which Roman soldiers would invest much time or energy." There was an animated discussion by those who had seen the movie and comments by those who had deliberately stayed away, not only because of the violence but because of the anti-Semitism.

They dwelt also upon the rough mockery of the Roman soldiers who, no doubt, had become hardened to human suffering. They could scarcely have had much personal animosity to this ragged scarecrow of a man, just another troublemaker to deal with.

"By now," remarked Melanie, "he was exhausted and scarcely able to carry the 'cross'. My reading suggests that the upright of the cross was left permanently implanted, a constant reminder of the fate of those who fell out with Roman power. The condemned person carried the crossbar which had a socket in its middle which allowed it to be placed onto the upright. So the cross was shaped like a capital T rather than the shape which is familiar to us." Webster agreed that he had read something of the same kind but wondered whether the word for "cross" allowed for this interpretation. "In fact," replied Melanie, rather surprised to know something that Webster hadn't discovered, "the word is 'stauros' and simply means a stake on which something can be hung. But let's not get delayed by these technicalities. Maybe we take refuge from the horror of it all by talking about how it was done."

They thought about this before moving on:

> Going out they met a Cyrenaean named Simon; whom they compelled to carry his cross, and so they came to a place called Golgotha, which means "Skull-ground." Here they gave him a mixture of wine and gall to drink, but having tasted it he refused to drink it.
>
> After crucifying him, they divided his garments among them by lot, and sat down there on guard. Over his head they placed a written statement of the charge against him: THIS IS JESUS THE KING OF THE JEWS.

They had read that the wine mixed with gall had some anaesthetic properties. But it wasn't clear why the soldiers would wish to lessen the pain. "Maybe someone in the crowd had pity on him," suggested Andrew, "although it would have been a daring act to step up to administer the potion. And why did he refuse it?" A pious opinion from the group suggested that he chose to take his punishment in full consciousness but the discussion was, as so often the case, inconclusive. Webster said, "I hadn't noticed until now the peculiar way of stating that Jesus was crucified. In a subordinate clause, 'After crucifying him, they divided his garments . . . ' Almost as though the dividing was the important thing!" Martha had the last word. "What about the placard? Someone must have brought it along. Surely no one prepared it on the spot. Did a Roman soldier go to that trouble just to taunt the crowd?" Interesting questions but no interesting answers, so time to move on:

> *At the same time two robbers were crucified with him, one at his right hand and the other at his left. And the passers-by reviled him. They shook their heads at him and said, "You who would pull down the Sanctuary and build a new one within three days, save yourself. If you are God's Son, come down from the cross."*
>
> *In like manner the High Priests also, together with the Scribes and the Elders, taunted him. "He saved others," they said, "himself he cannot save! He is the King of Israel! Let him now come down from the cross, and we will believe in him. His trust is in God: let God deliver him now, if he will have him; for he said, 'I am God's Son.'"*
>
> *Insults of the same kind were heaped on him even by the robbers who were being crucified with him.*

"Do you notice," asked Stephen, who had been reading the other Gospel accounts, " that there is no let up. No repentant thief, no kindly words addressed by Jesus to his mother and the 'Beloved Disciple', no prayer for forgiveness of his tormentors. The starkness of the account somehow adds to its horror." They sat in silence for a while, each preoccupied with their own thoughts. Reluctantly Melanie pushed ahead:

> *Now from noon until three o'clock in the afternoon there was darkness over the whole land; but about three o'clock Jesus cried out in a loud voice, "Eli, Eli, lama sabachthani?" that is to say, "My God, My God, why hast Thou forsaken me?"*
>
> *"The man is calling for Elijah," said some of the bystanders. One of them ran forthwith, and filling a sponge with sour wine put it on the end of a cane and offered it him to drink; while the rest said, "Let us see whether Elijah is coming to deliver him."*

Melanie gave Andrew the nod to amplify his earlier comment. "Traditionally, there were 'seven words from the Cross', all familiar utterances. But Matthew (and Mark) give only one. We all know it is the first verse of Psalm 22. But it's a bit ironic that the mocking 'His trust is in God; let God deliver him now, if he will have him' comes from the same Psalm." Al was needing to explore more deeply. "Yes, but what does it mean? Did he truly despair, even lose faith, at that moment? Had he been expecting divine intervention and now realized that it wouldn't come?" Melanie added, "We've read his predictions of the Passion. Surely he shouldn't have been surprised. Maybe the word and the event were two different things." They all looked puzzled by this last statement and she was glad that no one asked for elucidation!

"What about the darkness?" asked Martha. "Is there any record of an eclipse?" To her surprise, Stephen had found a calculation by two Oxford scientists, which indicated a lunar eclipse at about the right day, April 3, in the year 33 of the Christian era. Martha said that this reminded her of attempts to identify the Star of Bethlehem. They seemed to agree that the darkness over the land was symbolic of the darkness of the deed. Melanie reminded them of the tradition in the early Church and to Christians ever since, that the hours from noon to three on Good Friday have a special solemnity. "I remember as a kid spending three long hours in church. How I hated it! Just the worst time of the year. Too much, then; and too much, now."

So at last, it is over:

> *But Jesus uttered another loud cry and then yielded up his spirit.*
>
> *Immediately the curtain of the Sanctuary was torn in two from top to bottom: the earth quaked; the rocks split; the tombs opened; and many of God's people who were asleep in death awoke. And coming out of their tombs after Christ's resurrection they entered the holy city and showed themselves to many.*
>
> *As for the Captain and the soldiers who were with him keeping guard over Jesus, when they witnessed the earthquake and the other occurrences they were filled with terror, and exclaimed, "Assuredly he was God's Son."*

"What about these events?" asked Al. "Surely they are attempts to show the cosmic consequences of the death. And here are resurrections happening all over the place. Shouldn't they have waited until Sunday?" There was some discussion and the suggestion that the resurrections and the earthquake belonged to the next chapter. "After all," said Webster, "the guard are not assigned until the next day."

There was growing fatigue and time was running out so they needed to move on.

> *And there were a number of women there looking on from a distance, who had followed Jesus from Galilee ministering to his necessities; among them being Mary of Magdala, Mary the mother of James and Joses, and the mother of the sons of Zebedee.*
>
> *Towards sunset there came a wealthy inhabitant of Arimathea, named Joseph, who himself also had become a disciple of Jesus. He went to Pilate and begged to have the body of Jesus, and Pilate ordered it to be given to him. So Joseph took the body and wrapped it in a clean sheet of fine linen. He then laid it in his own new tomb which he had hewn in the solid rock, and after rolling a great stone against the door of the tomb he went home.*
>
> *Mary of Magdala and the other Mary were both present there, sitting opposite to the sepulchre.*

Melanie reminded them that, without the intervention of Joseph of Arimathea, the body of Jesus, an executed criminal, would have been dumped into the Valley of Hinnon. All part of the humiliation associated with crucifixion. Martha took them in a different direction. "The tomb has a womb-like character. He will be ready for new birth."

They were running overtime and Melanie quickly turned to the final section, with the comment, "The return of the Pharisees."

> *On the next day, the day after the Preparation, the High Priests and the Pharisees came in a body to Pilate. "Sir," they said, "we recollect that during his lifetime that impostor pretended that after two days he was to rise to life again. So give orders for the sepulchre to be securely guarded till the third day, for fear his disciples should come by night and steal the body, and then tell the people that he has come back to life; and so the last imposture will be more serious than the first."*
>
> *"You can have a guard," said Pilate: "go and make all safe, as best you can."*
>
> *So they went and made the sepulchre secure, sealing the stone besides setting the guard.*

Webster, as they gathered up their possessions to depart, could not restrain himself from two last comments. "They call Pilate, 'sir,' in Greek, 'kyrie'; and Pilate's response is sometimes translated, 'make all safe, if you can.' Nice irony in view of what is to come."

But they scarcely heard him. They had had enough.

Chapter 28

AT THE LAST MINUTE, on Easter Day, Melanie decided to accept Al's invitation to the chapel service. A crowded assembly, with many wheelchairs and others needing various helps in getting to the service. Rev. Ally was in fine form and the music, Melanie had to admit, was filled with hopefulness. Hymns sung with considerable energy brought back memories; *Jesus Christ is risen today* and *The strife is o'er, the victory won*. But the baptisms were the most memorable. An elderly couple, both in wheelchairs, residents at the hospital, and a single woman, one of the helpers. Ally skillfully incorporated elements of their life stories into her sermon, reminding all present of the occasions when need and opportunity coincide in surprising ways. This led seamlessly into similar themes from the Resurrection narratives. Against all expectations, Melanie found herself moved by what she was hearing, thinking of the opportunities which, thanks to Aunt Matty's unwelcome legacy, had come her way. And what of her needs? The question didn't go away. No balloons, no fireworks, but something very real.

She had time, that Easter Monday, to study Matthew's account of the resurrection. She wondered what to make of it. The trial, the death and burial were all within human experience but this, it was a mystery. She discovered that the total picture, from the other Gospels, was even more bewildering. On the one hand, the writers go to some pains to emphasize the reality of the event: he eats breakfast on the lakeshore with the disciples, and shows his wounds to doubting Thomas. This according to John. And Luke has his saying, "A spirit doesn't have flesh and bones as you see me have," and lets them touch him. Yet Mary Magdalene doesn't recognize him in the garden and the travelers on the road to Emmaus walk with him for an extended period, listening to him talk, yet unaware of his identity. And he has an uncanny way of appearing and disappearing. Melanie wondered if the Tuesday discussion would get bogged down in such questions. She was slightly reassured that Matthew's gospel avoided most of these difficulties.

When Tuesday came, she took the opportunity to thank all present for their active involvement and good preparation. "Here at last, we've reached the twenty eighth chapter. I thought we'd never get there and now . . ." she paused, struggling with her emotions. ". . . now, I'll be missing our Tuesday gatherings." Stephen reminded her of an unfinished agenda. "We're all hoping that you're back next year. We still have 'prayer' as a topic and, what was it? Christian Pacifism, I think. Didn't you agree to lead us?" He was only half-serious but she felt somehow flattered by his comment. "Let's not worry about next year," she replied. "There's work to be done!"

> *After the Sabbath, in the early dawn of the first day of the week, Mary of Magdala and the other Mary came to see the sepulchre. But to their amazement there had been a great earthquake; for an angel of the Lord had descended from Heaven, and had come and rolled back the stone, and was sitting upon it. His appearance was like lightning, and his raiment white as snow. For fear of him the guards trembled violently, and became like dead men. But the angel said to the women, "As for you, dismiss your fears. I know that it is Jesus that you are looking for—the crucified One. He is not here : he has come back to life, as he foretold. Come and see the place where he lay. And go quickly and tell his disciples that he has risen from the dead and is going before you into Galilee; there you shall see him. Remember, I have told you."*
>
> *They quickly left the tomb and ran, still terrified but full of unspeakable joy, to carry the news to his disciples. And then suddenly they saw Jesus coming to meet them. "Peace be to you," he said. And they came and clasped his feet, bowing to the ground before him. Then he said, "Dismiss all fear! Go and take word to my brethren to go into Galilee, and there they shall see me."*

The others had been doing their homework, too, and raised some of the same questions that had bothered Melanie. "But," said Al, "perhaps it's a piece of pious fiction, a happy ending to cheer us up." This started a lively discussion. "If it's fiction, it isn't well done," claimed Martha. "You might know that in patriarchal cultures, the testimony of women was not considered reliable. So why not have some more reliable witnesses?"

Then from Andrew, "Yes, and what about the time in the tomb? Do the arithmetic. It's no more than thirty hours and that world believed that a dead person's spirit lingered about for three full days. Keep him in the tomb for a week and then invent a resurrection if you want something truly miraculous." Al seemed somewhat satisfied with this but had another line of thought. "I read later on about the theory that the disciples stole the body. Suppose a few of them did, and the rest made up the story." Melanie suggested that they delay the discussion of the "stolen body" theory until the next section. Andrew drew attention to the fact that the women encounter Jesus in the garden. "But the men have to trudge back to Galilee. The other gospels seem to have a different set of encounters." Melanie could feel Webster itching to explore that theme but she intervened to push the discussion in a different direction. "What is the significance of Galilee, do you think?" Stephen suggested that it was a symbolic return to the place where it all began. "A sermon I heard at Easter proposed that encounter with Christ can be achieved when we return to the place where we first responded to the call 'Follow me'. That seemed to ring a bell for me." They remembered Stephen's account of his baptism and his annual commemoration. After a pause, Martha rounded off the discussion with the observation that women had been the first who proclaimed the resurrection. "It wasn't long before the men took over," she remarked.

Then onwards to the alternative explanation, concocted by others:

> While they went on this errand, some of the guards came into the city and reported to the High Priests every detail of what had happened. So the latter held a conference with the Elders, and after consultation with them they heavily bribed the soldiers, telling them to say, "His disciples came during the night and stole his body while we were asleep." "And if this," they added, "is reported to the Governor, we will satisfy him and screen you from punishment."
>
> So they took the money and did as they were instructed; and this story was noised about among the Jews, and is current to this day.

Webster supposed that the soldiers were temple guards who would have been responsible to the High Priest. They went back, in some fear over their failure to carry out their mandate. "Instead of punishment, they get a reward!" But Al wanted to continue with his question. "I still think that the theft theory is the most likely one." Andrew countered with the thought, "Would it be likely that Matthew would include such a rumor in his gospel. It would only perpetuate it." But Al wasn't easily put off. "Maybe the rumor was so strong that he needed to mention it and then explain it as a conspiracy." The conversation seemed to have reached an impasse. "We will move on," decided Melanie:

> As for the eleven disciples, they proceeded into Galilee, to the hill where Jesus had arranged to meet them. There they saw him and prostrated themselves before him. Yet some doubted. Jesus however came near and said to them, "All power in Heaven and over the earth has been given to me.
>
> Go therefore and make disciples of all the nations; baptize them into the name of the Father, and of the Son, and of the Holy Spirit; and teach them to obey every command which I have given you. And remember, I am with you always, day by day, until the close of the age."

She reminded them of the powerful influence of this section in motivating missionary endeavor. "If you Google, *Great Commission*, you get more than seven hundred thousand hits." Webster remarked that part of the reason why it is so popular is the fact that it is one of the very few places where such a clear mandate is given. "In all the epistles of the New Testament, the requirement for ordinary Christians to evangelize their neighbors is conspicuously absent. Some would argue this point," he admitted, " but it is very strange. Paul, for example, has advice on all manner of things relating to how Christians should live. But he doesn't ever tell them to 'make disciples'. That seems to be assigned to the apostles and to those specially gifted." There was a lively discussion on this. Andrew, in particular, was rather excited. "We're often told from the pulpit that we need to go about spreading the gospel. But none of us has much nerve for it. Maybe now I will go about feeling less guilty!"

Stephen reflected on the fact that, of all the world religions, only Christianity and Islam had this urge to convert others. "My Jewish friends find it a very alien idea. In fact, they rather resist the non-Jew who wishes to convert. Certainly they don't encourage it." Martha commented on this. "It's not only the Great Commission. It's the idea that unless you're a Christian, you're doomed. There was a lot of energy in that."

No one had raised the point concerning the possibility that this last section was added later. Melanie had read discussions about the formula, "... in the name of the Father and of the Son and of the Holy Spirit..." with theories that it came from the early church rather than from Jesus himself. She was rather relieved to avoid another inconclusive discussion. "It's been a shorter session than most and I suppose a summing up might be helpful. But I, for one don't have a clue where to start. What can one say about such a long journey, of the nativity, the baptism, the temptation? And the teaching and healing, the parables and the conflicts with the Pharisees? Of the Last Supper, the betrayal, the trial and crucifixion; and finally this mysterious resurrection? I guess we all carry away complicated responses." That seemed a lame way to end and she was grateful to Al who intervened. "We have met twenty nine times, by my count," he said. "Would it be possible to meet one last time? I would like you to be my guests for dinner next Tuesday at 6." They were all rather astonished at the thought that he would provide dinner for them all but eager and grateful to respond. Remarkably, all would be able to come.

Epilogue

They assembled together in Al's apartment, rather amazed that he would invite them all and half expecting beer and pizza. Their surprise was heightened when they saw a long table, with white cloth and all the accoutrements of fine dining. Al, having guided them up the steep staircase at the back of his bookstore, explained that, when his uncle had been proprietor, the upper level had been used as a storage area. There was a freight elevator, originally for books, now serving to transport the requirements for the evening. "Except that it isn't big enough for people, hence the climb."

A table by the window gave a variety of Australian wines for the meal. When their glasses were filled and they had taken their places at the table, Al was able to explain his sense that, having shared the journey through Matthew's Gospel, they should share a meal. He also mentioned that it was a belated thirty-fifth birthday party and that, since he had no family except in Australia, he was glad to share the occasion with friends. Predictably, they sang The Song; just as predictably, Stephen was able to inform them that "Happy Birthday" was still under copyright. "Maybe we should be paying someone royalties!" Considering this, Webster thought that they might end up in court and besought Melanie's opinion. She responded, "Royalties might apply to public performances but if you end up in court, I won't be much use, cowering there in the dock beside you. Anyway, considering the quality of our singing, we might more likely be sued by neighbors for breach of the peace." So the lighthearted conversation continued as three young women appeared, as if by magic, to begin serving the meal. "I thought lamb might do," said Al. "I hope that none of us are vegetarians."

As the meal progressed, the conversation came around to memories of the other Tuesday evenings and eventually Webster gained the attention of the group. He wished to propose a toast. "We all know what a difficult situation Melanie found herself in. Those first few meetings were a bit tense until we discovered that she brought a new style to leadership, a style that freed us up to ask the awkward questions and to give up the corny jokes. And, of course, having Al was a great bonus, although I think he knew more than he let on! But it was Melanie's openness and the sense that she was engaged in a personal search that made all the difference. So I wish to propose a toast: to Melanie, may she never cease from her explorings!" They raised their glasses with enthusiasm and then waited for Melanie's response. "Webster knows his Eliot," she began. "'... and the end of all our exploring will be to arrive where we started and know the place for the first time.' Not quite true for me, I think; the place where I have arrived is rather different from where I started. You might remember my resentment towards Aunt Matty that I expressed rather strongly at that first meeting. So where am I now? In a bit of a wilderness, I think. And no John the Baptist in sight!" She paused and the room was rather silent. "Anyway, I thank you for the kind words and the toast." She struggled to find the right words. "Do you recall the first meeting when I ran out of things to say and I asked you to speak of your expectations? Does anyone wish to reflect on the experience of journeying through Matthew?" The response was rather predictable and, she thought, exaggerated her role in all that had happened. Then Al spoke up, in such a way that she guessed that he had been preparing for such a moment. "This has been a remarkable experience for me. You may know that I was raised in a household where hostility to Christian faith was very strong. My experience with the men's group last year helped alleviate some of that. But it wasn't until I went through Matthew with this group that it began to make sense. I suppose that when we began, if anyone asked me if I was a Christian, I would have given an uncertain response. Now that has changed." He paused to pull a card from his pocket. "Recently I came across a piece from a writer named Will Willimon which expresses my situation rather well. Willimon asks, 'When did the story of Jesus come to illumine and make sense of my story in such a way that my little life became part of the larger adventure called the Gospel?' My answer would be 'sometime during our Tuesday sessions.' I have Melanie to thank." Again there was a pause, until Melanie replied, "It's ironic, isn't it, that I am the one giving the 'uncertain response' concerning Christian faith. It has been my belief that Aunt Matty set this up in the hope that I would find faith; she couldn't have anticipated that her scheme had rather unexpected consequences."

The conversation then lightened again and the evening came to a pleasant conclusion, an appropriate ending to their times together. Melanie was the last to leave and she paused on the doorstep to remark to Al, "Do you remember the first time we met, after that first session? You said that you were looking for Mr. Right. So you found him!" Al reminded her of her response on that occasion: that she knew the feeling and hoped that her Mr. Right might not be the same as his. "It's ironic, the way that piece of chatter now takes a different meaning," he concluded. "Maybe we will end up with the same Mr. Right, after all."

With that, they parted and Melanie went out into the darkening streets to find her way home.